FOUR GREEK PLAYS

KU-258-588

THE
PAUL HAMLYN
LIBRARY

———— ◆ ————

DONATED BY
THE PAUL HAMLYN
FOUNDATION
TO THE
BRITISH MUSEUM

———— ◆ ————

opened December 2000

PHL

54060000064864

Also available or forthcoming from BCP:

Aeneas: Virgil's Epic Retold for Younger Readers, E. Frenkel

In the *Inside the Ancient World* series:

Aeneas and the Roman Hero, R. Deryck Williams
*Athenian Democracy, Robin Barrow
*Athenian Society, Jennifer Gibbon
*Cicero and Rome, David Taylor
*Greek and Roman Education, Robin Barrow
*The Greek and Roman Stage, David Taylor
*Homer, Martin Thorpe
Penelope to Poppaea, Anne Haward
Roman Comedy, Kenneth McLeish
Roman Provincial Administration, John Richardson
Roman Society, David Taylor
Slavery in Ancient Rome, M. Massey and P. Moreland
*Socrates and Athens, Meg Parker
Vitruvius: Architect and Engineer, Alexander McKay

*Denotes books which are especially suited to GCSE or studies at a comparable 16+ level. The remainder may be useful at that level, but can also be used by students on more advanced courses.

882. 01 MCL

THE BRITISH MUSEUM
WITHDRAWN
THE PAUL HAMLYN LIBRARY

FOUR GREEK PLAYS

Sophocles:
OEDIPUS THE KING
ANTIGONE

Aristophanes:
THE ACHARNIANS
PEACE

Translated and adapted by
KENNETH McLEISH

Bristol Classical Press

First published by Longmans, Green and Co. Ltd, 1964

This edition published in 1998 by
Bristol Classical Press
an imprint of
Gerald Duckworth & Co. Ltd
61 Frith Street
London W1V 5TA

Reprinted 1999

© 1964 by Kenneth McLeish

All rights reserved. No part of this publication
may be reproduced, stored in a retrieval system, or
transmitted, in any form or by any means, electronic,
mechanical, photocopying, recording or otherwise,
without the prior permission of the publisher.

A catalogue record for this book is available
from the British Library

ISBN 1-85399-583-5

Printed in Great Britain by
Booksprint

CONTENTS

INTRODUCTION

1. THE THEATRES OF ANCIENT GREECE

(i) The place and time of performance:

Theatres in Ancient Greece were very different from those of today. Modern theatres are roofed-in buildings designed like boxes, with all the seats facing the stage—comfortable, well-upholstered seats which can be reserved in advance. But Greek theatres were very different. For one thing, they were all out of doors; in a country with such a warm and reliable climate, many of the things *we* do inside could take place in the open air—for example, sacrifices and feasts were usually held outside, and the Assembly (the equivalent of our Parliament) was held in a special open-air meeting place —which explains how, at the beginning of *The Acharnians*, Dikaiopolis can bring it to an abrupt end by "arranging" for a shower of rain.

A modern play is designed primarily as entertainment: it lasts between two and three hours, and is usually performed in the evening. But again, things were different in Greece. Greek plays were part of a religious celebration: the day began with a sacrifice, went on with various entertainments (including a drama competition); and ended with a feast. There were only a few theatrical occasions in the year: in Athens there were two important festivals lasting several days, and a number of shorter ones. And these were the *only* occasions on which plays were performed. The audience paid nothing for their seats, and the money for the performance was provided by some rich man with an eye on forthcoming elections. This meant that productions were very lavish and expensive; but, since these men believed that they could most impress the people by providing constant novelty, they were only interested in newly-written plays. Therefore, except in a very few cases, a play received only one performance, and was not staged again for several years— a run of months, or years, such as we are used to, would be an unheard-of thing for an ancient dramatist.

During the religious feasts—public holidays, when the whole population of the city came to the theatre—the performances lasted all day. On each day of the festival three tragedies and one less-serious play were performed, and on the last day specially elected judges awarded prizes for the most popular plays. (These prizes, usually consisting of a barrel of wine, or a pig, or a couple of chickens, were clearly more valuable for the prestige they brought than in themselves. But a successful dramatist always won great fame and honour in the city: Sophocles and Aristophanes, for example, were two of the most respected men in Athens, and no doubt many copies of their plays would be circulated whenever they were victorious in a competition.) Before Sophocles' time, the author generally took the leading part in his own play; but Sophocles himself had a very weak voice, and had to be satisfied with being his own director, a custom that was followed by most later dramatists.

In the theatre, seats were allotted in order of importance. Since the performances were part of a religious festival, the priests were given the best seats; behind them special places were reserved for the officials of the city and ambassadors from foreign states; and behind them sat the generals and other important citizens, with the ordinary townsfolk at the back. Within these restrictions, however, seats were unreserved, and, because people were afraid of losing their places if they moved, it was customary for each member of the audience to bring his own refreshments—and cushions, too, since the majority of seats were made of stone.

(ii) The theatres themselves:

The diagram on p. x gives a good impression of what a Greek theatre looked like. The audience sat on tiers of seats built up on (or carved out of) a conveniently-shaped hillside. In front of these seats was a large levelled-off area about the size of a tennis-court, and shaped like an oval. This was called the 'dancing-place'.[1] Behind this, facing the audience, was a low stage about a foot high, with no curtain and no wings: just a platform roughly two-thirds the length of the "dancing-place" and about eight feet wide. Behind this was the back wall of the stage, a wooden building about ten feet high that ran the full length of the stage. Its front was made of canvas over a wooden frame, and was painted to resemble rocks, or trees, or the front of a building—exactly like the backcloth in a modern theatre. In Oedipus the King and Antigone it was painted like the front of a palace; in The Acharnians it depicted a city street, and in Peace it was simply painted with rocks and boulders. The roof of this stage-building was flat, and was sometimes used (as in The Acharnians and Peace) for the performance of aerial scenes (see pp. 119 and 161).

---

[1] The Greek word for dancing-place was orchestra, and it is interesting that the modern word "orchestra" means the people who perform (originally in the chorus-part of a theatre, the pit), and not the place where they perform.

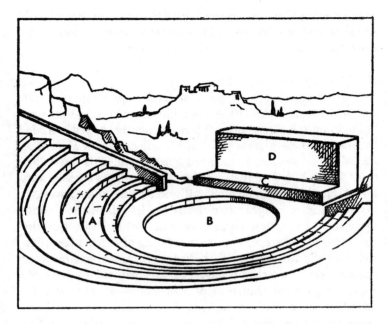

A. Audience seats. B. The "dancing-place".

C. The Stage. D. The Stage-building.

2. THE ACTORS AND THE CHORUS

(i) The actors:

In the Greek theatre—as in Shakespeare's time—all the actors were men. They wore masks to represent the characters they were playing, and moved in a stiff, stylised manner. The modern method of acting, which is called "naturalistic" because it imitates the way people speak and move in real life, would have seemed incongruous and laughable to a Greek audience: they expected their actors, particularly in tragedy, to perform in a magnificent, ballet-like manner. There were usually three principal actors, and all the speaking parts were divided between them: they were the *Protagonist* (in *Oedipus the King* he would play Oedipus), the *Deuteragonist* (who would play Jocasta, the Priest, the Messenger and the Shepherd), and the *Tritagonist* (who would play Creon, Tiresias and the Servant). The fact that there were only three actors explains why there are never more than three people talking on the stage at any one time, and often only two (so that the third actor can change his mask, ready to come on in a different role). The other people on the stage—guards, servants, suppliants, and the other non-speaking parts—were probably played by apprentice actors, learning their trade. They had a technical name—"Silent masks"—and helped to "dress" the very long stage, which would otherwise have dwarfed the three leading players.

Although in comedy great numbers of props were called for, in tragedy very few props and not much scenery were used: the audience was more interested in what the actors said than in what they did. They came in through a door in the front of the stage building (which in *Oedipus the King* and *Antigone* represents the great doors of a palace, and in *The Acharnians* the door of Dikaiopolis' house), and they had their dressing-rooms either in the stage-building itself, or in huts built behind it. What they did on the stage was not too different from what happens in a modern play: the characters were fewer, and the action slower and more stylised, but the methods of performance were basically the same.

(ii) The Chorus:

However, the big difference is not in what took place on the stage itself, but in what went on in front of it, in the *dancing-place*. (There is nothing like this in the modern "picture-frame" theatre, though some modern designers are now building theatres modelled on those of ancient Greece). In the dancing-place of a Greek theatre were grouped the CHORUS. They were normally 15 in number—though in extravagant productions there could be many more—and they had a very important part to play in the performance. The action of the play was divided into sections—five in a tragedy, three or four in a comedy—and after each of these scenes the Chorus performed an interlude to the accompaniment of a flute, and moving in grave, ritual patterns to the rhythm of the words. These choral "odes", as they were called, neatly divided the action, provided a necessary relaxation of tension, and also gave the actors time to prepare themselves for the next scene. In the old days the Chorus were the most important people in the play; but by Sophocles' time their part had become very much smaller.

The function of the Chorus is considerably different in tragedy and comedy. In tragedy their odes are generally used to comment on what has been said in each scene; they are not part of the play itself (in the sense that they do not advance the action), but stand aside from it, commenting on what is happening and providing the "ideal reaction" to each succeeding scene. However, in addition to their odes, which are performed entirely in the dancing-place, the Chorus sometimes take part in the actual scenes as well. When this happens, the Chorus-leader goes up to the stage and joins the actors—but he still adds very little to the action of the play. His duty in the scenes is to play the part of an ordinary bystander, a man in the street: look at what the Chorus says in the *scenes* of *Oedipus* or *Antigone*—he rarely expresses opinions of his own, and his main function seems to be to agree with the character who is speaking, or tell him things he doesn't already know.

In comedy, however, the role of the Chorus is very different. Their speeches are not reserved for commenting on the action, or reacting like ordinary people, but form, instead, an integral part of what is happening. They are usually violently opposed to whatever the hero wants to do, and his first task in the play is to win them over to his side. After they *are* convinced, they assist him in arguing with and defeating the numerous beggars and swindlers who flock round him after he has won his victory: their odes, though performing a similar function to those in tragedy, are shorter and occur more frequently, often in the middle of the scenes themselves. And in addition to all this they have a unique section of each comedy to themselves, the *Parabasis*. In this long ode, which comes in the middle of the play, after the hero has won his victory, and before he is besieged by all the people eager to share his good fortune, the Chorus step outside the action, and address the audience directly, telling them what a fine man the author is, and exhorting them to award him the first prize. Aristophanes very often uses the Parabasis for outspoken criticism of rival playwrights and the people he is satirising: the Parabasis of *Peace* (p. 178) is a good example of this plain speaking.

It will be seen, then, that there is a big difference between the choruses of a tragedy and those of a comedy. But whatever their function, they are a unique feature of Greek drama, something which at first strikes our modern ears as a little strange, but which, once you grow accustomed to the idea, lends a depth and splendour to Greek plays that is lacking in the looser and more immediately striking construction of contemporary drama.

3. THE ATHENS OF SOPHOCLES AND ARISTOPHANES

(i) "The Fifty Years":
At the time when Sophocles and Aristophanes were writing (i.e., the last 60 years of the 5th century B.C.), there was no civilisation greater than that of Greece. The civilisations of Egypt and China had passed the time of their greatest achievements, and the equally magnificent civilisation of the Minoans, the people of Crete, had been completely destroyed. The mighty Persian Empire, which controlled practically all of what is now the Middle East and Russia, invaded Greece at the beginning of the 5th century, and was beaten back, leaving the Greeks to enjoy a period of unparalleled prosperity. By conquering Persia, the greatest military power in the world, they had proved their ability in war; and now, with fifty years of peace ahead of them, they turned their attention to other matters : most of the great discoveries in Mathematics, Philosophy and the Arts owe their origin to the Greeks of this Golden Age. It cannot be overstressed that no nation at any time has ever achieved so much—in every field of activity, from athletics to poetry, from architecture and shipbuilding to oratory—in such a brief period of time. The people sensed that nothing like this had ever happened in history before, and gave their own time the proud title of " The Fifty Years " (or, as we would say, " *The* Fifty Years ").

At this time the country was split up into a large number of small states, each consisting of a single city and the surrounding countryside. This was the most sensible way of dividing Greece, since it is criss-crossed by high (and, in those days, practically impassable) mountain-ranges, which cut the country into hundreds of small valleys, each ruled as a separate kingdom. Many of these city-states, like Thebes and Corinth, were—or had been—wealthy and prosperous: and the greatest of them all was Athens. In this city, which had led the defence of Greece against the Persians, the activities characteristic of the whole nation were seen at their most perfect: Athenian generals, historians and dramatists were the greatest in Greece; her trade was more widespread, and her wealth greater, than that of any other city. The people of Athens believed—quite rightly—that there was no finer city in the world, and that their system of democracy was the best possible way of being governed. And, since they enjoyed military supremacy as well, no one else seriously challenged this belief throughout the whole of "The Fifty Years".

It is to this period of prosperity that Sophocles belongs. His was the generation that defeated the Persians; he was a wealthy and respected man, and a staunch supporter of the principles of democracy and stability which had made the city great. This is one reason for his enormous popularity in his own day; another is the fact that when a Greek city was prosperous and at peace, the Arts flourished as at no other time. Everyone in Athens was deeply interested in the theatre: it was, after all, part of their religious life. And Sophocles' plays, many of them dealing with the myths of days more troubled than their own—and full of comparisons between, for example, the tumultuous history of the autocratic Kings of Thebes, and the peace and freedom of the Athenian democracy—found a willing and enthusiastic audience in the somewhat self-satisfied citizens of his own beloved city.

(ii) Athens and Sparta:

However, things were not to remain so happy for ever. Another state, Sparta, had been growing in power and organisation throughout the century. Sparta was entirely devoted to military glory : her soldiers were the toughest in Greece, and every man in the city was in the army—nothing mattered to a Spartan but military excellence. Sparta was a totalitarian state : no one was allowed a private life; everything was held in common, and there was no freedom of speech. And as her power grew, it was natural that she should challenge the might of Athens, and seek to become herself the leading power in Greece—particularly since Athens' democratic form of government must have been quite incomprehensible to the people of this rigidly-controlled and army-dominated state.

For years the Spartans and Athenians each made their preparations, forming alliances and building up their armies and fleets. Then, in 431 B.C., the Spartans struck, invading the countryside round Athens. They were repulsed, with difficulty : but the following year they invaded again, and again were driven back. This happened several times, without either side gaining any real advantage. But one result of the invasions was that the inhabitants of the surrounding country fled for safety into Athens : the city filled with refugees, and plague soon followed, caused partly by over-crowding and partly by lack of food due to the Spartans' blockade of Athenian trade routes.

And although Athens hung grimly on for no less than 27 years, without admitting defeat, all her wealth and prosperity drained away. She survived plague, siege, over-crowded conditions, starvation, and the exploitation of the people by unscrupulous generals (like Lamachos, in *Peace*) and rascally politicians (like Cleon, in *The Acharnians*)—but even a state as great as she had been could not hold out for ever, and when she eventually admitted defeat, in 404 B.C., her might was completely broken, and her people weary and spiritless.

Throughout these years of war, siege, and uneasy peace constantly broken by new attacks, the playwright Aristophanes produced comedy after comedy, full of savage mockery of the wicked politicians and grasping generals who were draining away the city's greatness. He tried to rouse the people by reminding them of their former glory, how they had routed the Persians only 60 years before; in both *The Acharnians* and *Peace* (by contrasting the happiness of men willing to rouse themselves and take steps to rescue themselves from their misery, with the plight of the oppres-sed and apathetic people who watched his plays), he attempted what rogues like Cleon and Lamachos refused to do : to rouse the people, and bring back their will to end the war. But no single man, not even Aristophanes—undoubt-edly one of the greatest satirists of all time—could prevent the inevitable : the city fell, and he himself survived her fall by some twenty years, writing careful, frightened plays with all the old political fire gone from them, a disillusioned, embittered man.

This is the background to the four plays in this volume : for Sophocles, a time of great prosperity and security, offer-ing a striking contrast to the tragic themes of most of his plays; for Aristophanes, a city torn by the greatest conflict it had ever known, a conflict which, at the time of *The Acharnians* and *Peace* (425 and 421), was already without hope: no end was in sight, and the people had lost the proud spirit that had made them great, the spirit that had routed the Persian hordes at the battle of Marathon, and made possible the glory of "The Fifty Years".

Translator's Note

Since these translations are principally intended for young readers and those making their first acquaintance with Greek drama, I have tried to remove from the plays as many barriers to immediate understanding as possible. In particular, passages of abstruse mythology—and, for other reasons, some of Aristophanes' more scatological references—have been cut, and some other sections (notably the choruses) have been paraphrased or—occasionally—rewritten entirely. Purists who think this approach undesirable, will find fuller and more literal versions of the plays readily available elsewhere; it is however hoped that the readers for whom these translations are mainly intended will find in them some of the spirit, if not all of the letter, that has made Greek drama for so long a lively and important part of our literary heritage.

I

OEDIPUS THE KING

NOTE

This play, like *Antigone*, deals with the family of Labdacus, who ruled the city of Thebes at the time of the Homeric heroes (*c.* 1000 B.C.). The story begins with Labdacus' son Laius and his queen Jocasta. They had a son, but before he was born the God Apollo prophesied that he would kill his father and marry his mother. Horrified by this prophecy, the King and Queen decided to have the baby put to death: and when he was only three days old, he was exposed and left to die on the desolate slopes of Mount Cithaeron.

After this Laius ruled peacefully and happily for some 25 years. Then one day he felt the need to go to Delphi, the temple of Apollo, and consult the oracle once more. He set off with a small party of servants; but he never reached Apollo's temple, for on the way he quarrelled at a crossroads with a lone traveller, and he and all but one of his servants were killed.

Soon afterwards Oedipus arrived in Thebes. He found the city in a state of terror: for, soon after Laius had left for Delphi, the Sphinx, a terrible and apparently unconquerable monster, had come to Thebes and posed the people a riddle— and every day on which they failed to find the answer she took one of the young girls of the city and devoured her. This was the riddle:

Four-legs in the morning, two at noon,
Three-legs again in the evening;
Walks on land and doesn't sink in sea;
Strongest with two legs, weakest with four—
What is it?

—and no one in the city, not even the wisest of the counsellors, could find the correct answer.

In their desperate plight they begged Oedipus to help them. After some days of thought, whether helped by the Gods or by his own efforts, he managed to solve the riddle, and defeat the Sphinx. *Four-legs in the morning*—crawling, as a baby; *two-legs at noon*—walking upright, as a youth; *three-legs in the evening*—walking with the help of a stick, in old age. The rest follows easily enough, and the answer is MAN.

Oedipus was acclaimed as the saviour of Thebes; and, as word had reached the city of Laius' tragic death—though no one knew who had killed him—the people begged Oedipus to marry Queen Jocasta and become their King. He did so; in the course of time, four children were born to him and Jocasta : Eteocles and Polynices, his sons, and Antigone and Ismene, his daughters. With the help of the Queen and her brother, the Lord Creon, Oedipus ruled justly and well; the city prospered, and no one had a thought to spare for the old, dead King. No one, that is, except the Gods. Apollo had not forgotten Laius, or the prophecy that had been made to him. In order that the people of Thebes should send a messenger to Delphi to ask for his help, and so that in this way the whole story could come to light, it was necessary for some terrible affliction to come upon the city. Accordingly, Apollo sent a frightful plague to torment Thebes.

At this point the story of OEDIPUS THE KING begins . . .

OEDIPUS THE KING

Characters:

OEDIPUS, *the King of Thebes*
JOCASTA, *his wife, the Queen*
CREON, *her brother*
TIRESIAS, *a blind prophet*
PRIEST
MESSENGER
SHEPHERD
SERVANT
ANTIGONE ⎫
ISMENE ⎭ *daughters of Oedipus, young children still*

CHORUS *of Theban elders*[1]

Guards, servants, suppliants, boy leading Tiresias, etc.

[1] Note: the choral odes, and all other choral parts, should be spoken by the full Chorus; but where the Chorus take part in the ordinary dialogue, their part should be taken by a single voice.

OEDIPUS THE KING

SCENE ONE

The city of Thebes, once a prosperous town in the middle of a fertile and beautiful plain, has been smitten by a terrible plague, which is drying up the soil and withering the crops, slaughtering the cattle and decimating the townspeople. In their agony and distress they remember how their king, Oedipus, saved them from the Sphinx—and now, seeking his help once more, they are gathering together before the great gates of the palace, thronging the courtyard, carrying green vine-branches to show that they come as suppliants. The sound of lamenting fills the city, and word has reached Oedipus of his people's plea that he should help them. The crowd wait anxiously for news before the palace; suddenly there is a fanfare, the great doors are flung open, and King OEDIPUS *comes out on to the marble steps.*

OEDIPUS: People of Thebes—my children—what does it
    mean,
    This weeping crowd at the palace gate? What brings
    You here? And why are you carrying vine-branches?
    The city is filled with the fumes of incense,
    With muttered prayers, and the groans of a people in
    torment.
    I have not sent out servants to question you:
    I have come myself, Oedipus the King, to hear
    What it is you are seeking.

He beckons to the PRIEST *to stand forward.*

You, sir: you seem fitted
By age and wisdom to speak for them all. What is it?
What do they want of me? Are they afraid? In need?
Tell me what is troubling you: I am the King,
And I shall do what I can to help my people.
A man would need to have ears of stone, to hear
And not to heed this bitter lamenting.
PRIEST: My lord, I speak for all who are gathered here:
For those too young to walk unhelped; for those
Of us who are bent and slow with age; for the priests
Of the city and the pick of our young fighting men.
We have come here, while others wait in the market-
place,
And others are praying at Ismenos' shrine, or in
The two great temples of our lady Athene.
OEDIPUS: What are they praying for? What has brought
you here?
PRIEST: Sir, you must know how sick the city lies,
How we are choking and drowning in a sea of misery:
Our crops are withered, our cattle dead in their stalls,
Our women barren, and all our hope destroyed.
Plague has settled on the city like a fire,
Consuming everything that lies before it—
Soon the streets will be gaunt and empty; soon
Hell's jaws will gape to swallow us alive.
In our agony we have turned again to you, my lord:
You have led us through times of wealth and plenty,
And in days of horror when the Gods turned against us.
When the Sphinx tormented us, you came
To break her spell, and give us our life again.
That is why we are turning to you now, Oedipus:
We have come to beg you to cure our misery, to end

7

Our agony, and find some way to help us.
We have hailed you as our saviour once before—
Let no one say that you raised us up once,
Only to cast us down again ! My lord,
Help us as you helped before ! Help
Your people, or you will rule a city of empty stones !

OEDIPUS: My children, this plea for help was not unex-
pected.
I know how bitterly you are suffering—
And yet I know that none of you is plunged
So deep in suffering as I, your King:
Your grief is single, and strikes each man
Once only, for himself and those he loves;
But the King's grief is all men's grief—your pain
And suffering touch me as well, and I am torn
With anguish for your sake. I was not asleep,
Or deaf to your requests: I have long known
The city's agony; I have lain awake
And frightened the grey dawn with troubled thoughts,
Searching the means to end my people's misery.
There was one way only, and I have followed it:
I have sent Creon, brother of my dearest Queen,
To Delphi, to Apollo's shrine, to ask
The God what I must do to save the city.
This was the day I hoped for his return—
Today I hoped for news. But he has not returned,
And his lateness troubles me. I swear to you,
Whatever the advice he brings from God,
I shall obey it gladly, fair or sad.

PRIEST: My lord, we thank you for this promise; no man
could offer more. And look: they've just brought word
that Creon has returned, and that he's coming here !

OEDIPUS: Yes, I see him—and he's smiling! God grant his news is good!

PRIEST: It must be: he's crowned with laurel, bright with berries, as a token of good tidings!

There is a fanfare, and CREON, *the King's brother-in-law, comes hurrying in. He kneels before* OEDIPUS, *who greets him warmly.*

OEDIPUS: My lord Creon, you're welcome back to Thebes.

CREON: Sir, I thank you.

OEDIPUS: What news have you brought from Delphi? Good or bad?

CREON: Good, my lord: the God has shown us the way to rid ourselves of the plague.

OEDIPUS *eagerly:* What is it? What must we do?

CREON: There's a pollution hanging over the country and causing the plague, an unclean thing fattening itself on our barren fields—and we must drive it out!

OEDIPUS: A pollution? What? And how can we rid ourselves of it?

CREON: By finding and punishing a murderer—it's the shedding of unlawful blood that's brought plague upon us!

OEDIPUS: Whose blood? Who was murdered?

CREON: Laius, my lord: Laius the old King. We must avenge him, and bring his murderers to justice.

OEDIPUS: But where *are* they? How can we find them now, so many years afterwards?

CREON: They're here, in Thebes itself—or so the God told me.

OEDIPUS: Where was Laius murdered? Here, in the

9

palace, or in the fields—or somewhere out of the country? Does anyone know?

CREON: He left Thebes to go to Delphi and ask the God's advice, and never came back!

OEDIPUS: Was anyone with him? Did anyone witness the murder? Can no one give us any information?

CREON: No: all his companions died with him, except one—and *he* ran away in terror, and can only tell us one thing with certainty—

OEDIPUS: What? It may be the clue we need!

CREON: He said the King was murdered by a band of robbers—not one man, but many.

OEDIPUS: But how would robbers dare to attack the King? . . . unless someone in Thebes had bribed them . . .

CREON: That occurred to us, too. But the city was in such confusion, at the time of the murder, that no one made any further inquiries.

OEDIPUS *incredulously:* No one made any inquiries? Into the death of the King? What "confusion" was great enough to prevent anyone investigating such a hideous crime?

CREON *simply:* The Sphinx—we'd troubles here at home to think about, before any that were further away.

OEDIPUS: The Sphinx? . . . I see. And so it's left to me to start the search for the murderers afresh . . . (*decisively*) Very well: I shall try to find them—I owe it to Thebes, to the memory of the old King, and to myself: for whoever killed Laius may well decide next to turn his hand against *me!*

He turns to address the waiting crowd.

10

People of Thebes, your plea is answered! I swear, before you all, to rid the city of this plague! With God's help we'll conquer it—or be conquered ourselves!

He goes into the palace, accompanied by CREON.

PRIEST: My children, this promise was what we came to seek. Let us pray now, that Phoebus Apollo, who has told us how to end the plague, may himself come down and help us!

The CHORUS, *who have been acting as suppliants, now return to their positions in the dancing-place, and sing an ode asking the Gods for help.*

CHORUS A:

It is no longer with weapons of war,
But the creeping horror of foul corruption,
The shrieks of men dying in twisted agony,
That the Lord of Death is slowly choking us.

CHORUS B:

No buds, no promise of new life in the meadowland:
The standing crops, and the unborn seeds, are dead;
The women of Thebes are screaming in a childbirth
That will bring no child to end its bitter pain.

CHORUS A:

Like geese on the wing, seeking the warm south,
The souls of our people flit in the darkened sky,
Flocking to find the dark edge of the evening,
Death's halls, and the courts of the nameless Dead.

CHORUS B:

But Apollo has spoken! His word has come,
Bright as a blazing beacon to gladden us;
His golden bow is bent—his arrows are flying
To put to flight our sombre, silent enemy!

CHORUS A:

    O Lord Apollo, come to help us! Come, and end
    The gloomy litanies of Death! Artemis, come!
    Bacchus, patron of Thebes, lord of the pinewood, come!
    Come down to us: strike terror in our enemies!

CHORUS B:

    We are choking to death in the cruel grasp
    Of Night's cold fingers—but our help is near:
    For the Gods, too, hate the Nameless One,
    And are rising to join us, to break his fearful spell!

*

SCENE TWO

The scene is the same. To the sound of another fanfare, OEDIPUS *comes out to address the people once again.*

OEDIPUS: My people, you came to me to ask for help—and I shall help you, if you listen to me, and do as I command you. Before today I knew nothing of this murder: I was a stranger here when the crime was committed, and no one's ever spoken of it since then. But the time for silence is past: if anyone does know anything, he must tell me, now! As Thebes' newest citizen, and her King, I make you this proclamation: any man who knows who murdered Laius the son of Labdacus, must come forward now, and tell me everything. If the murderer himself is here, but is afraid to admit his guilt, for fear of punishment, I order him to speak—he won't be tortured or executed, and will suffer nothing worse

12

than banishment. Finally, if any one of you saw Laius' murderer, and it was someone from a foreign country, say so, now. Any man who helps to solve this mystery will be well rewarded—and everyone in Thebes will honour him as the saviour of the city.

It may be, however, that someone's hiding what he knows, because he's afraid, either for himself or for one of his friends. If there *is* such a man among you, I urge him to take these words to heart: as Lord and King of Thebes, I solemnly command all her citizens, when they find him, to banish him for ever. No one must speak to him or offer him shelter; no one must take him into their house, or invite him to share their feasts or sacrifices! You must cast him out: you must spurn him, and banish him from Thebes!

So much for anyone who conceals information. As for the murderer himself—whether he's one single man, or a member of a gang—I pray that he may live a tormented, accursed and friendless life, and die in misery! And I add myself to this curse: if the murderer's found under my roof, and I allow him shelter there, knowing what he's done, I pray that I may suffer the same fate as I've decreed for others!

This, then, is my proclamation. And it's your duty, citizens of Thebes, to see that it's carried out—it's your duty to the God, to me, and to your country, which is wasting away before your eyes! I'm the only man Laius has left to avenge him—and I swear to search for his murderers as eagerly as if it had been my own father that they'd killed! It's up to you to help me: if you don't, I pray that all the agonies you're suffering now—blighted crops, barren wives, starving children—may be doubled, and that you may die friendless and miserable! But if you *do* help me, I promise that we won't be fighting alone: Justice and all the Gods are on our side!

There is a moment of hushed silence, and then the Leader of the CHORUS *speaks, a little hesitantly.*

CHORUS: My lord, this is a terrible curse—but a just one! I myself can tell you nothing: *I* didn't murder Laius, and I didn't see who did! . . . There's only one sure way to find the criminal—

OEDIPUS *eagerly:* What?

CHORUS: Apollo ordered this inquiry—couldn't we ask *him* who it is we're looking for?

OEDIPUS: We could *ask* him, yes: but so far he's told us nothing, and no one can make him speak against his will!

CHORUS: There *is* one way—

OEDIPUS: What's that?

CHORUS: Tiresias, his prophet! *He* might be the man to ask! *He* might have clearer information!

OEDIPUS: Yes: Creon suggested him, too. I've sent twice to fetch him—I'm surprised they haven't brought him yet.

CHORUS *musingly:* There's not much else I can tell you . . . of course, people said things, at the time of the murder . . .

OEDIPUS *eagerly:* What? What did they say?

CHORUS: It was only gossip: nothing of any importance.

OEDIPUS: Everything's important that may lead to the truth! What did they say?

CHORUS: There was a rumour that he was killed by travellers—

OEDIPUS: Yes, so I heard. But no one can tell us anything more definite!

CHORUS: My lord, if anyone *does* know, and has been too frightened to say so, your curse will certainly make him speak out now! (*eagerly*) And look—here comes the prophet!

OEDIPUS: At last!

CHORUS: If anything *is* known, Tiresias will have heard it! Nothing escapes him, blind though he is!

TIRESIAS is led in by his BOY. OEDIPUS goes to greet him.

OEDIPUS: My lord Tiresias, we know there's nothing in Heaven or earth that escapes you, even though your eyes are sightless! You must, therefore, have heard of the city's anguish, and how no one but you can help us end it. You must know, too, how Apollo answered our questions, telling us to find Laius' murderers and punish them. My lord, if you've heard anything—if the birds[1], or sacred offerings, have brought you any news, tell us now! You'll be helping yourself, your city, your King, and everything this murder has polluted! We're in your hands—no one else can save us!

But TIRESIAS seems crushed by the weight of some great sorrow, some knowledge too dreadful to reveal. When he speaks, it is slowly, and as if to himself.

TIRESIAS *bitterly*: How useless wisdom is when it only leads to evil! I should have remembered that sooner—I should never have come at all!

[1] In Greek religion, the cries of birds, and the appearance of the livers of sacrificed animals, were used as a basis for the determination of omens and prophecies.

OEDIPUS: My lord, what is it that's troubling you?

TIRESIAS *vehemently:* Sire, send me back! Send me back *now*, back where I came from!

OEDIPUS *taken aback:* What? Think, my lord! Think what you're asking! You're the only person who can save the city—your *own* city!—and you want me to send you back without asking your advice! Why? What is it that you know?

TIRESIAS: Oedipus, I beg you: don't make me speak! *Your* oaths and promises will turn out badly enough—I won't make matters worse by speaking out as well!

OEDIPUS: Make matters worse? What do you mean? What are you hiding from us?

TIRESIAS *does not answer.*

Speak, man! We're at our wits' end: we beseech you to help us!

TIRESIAS *desperately:* You don't realise—any of you—the danger you're in!

OEDIPUS: What are you talking about? What danger?

Again TIRESIAS *makes no reply.*

Tiresias, the city's slowly dying of plague! Will you betray us now, when no one else can help us?

TIRESIAS: It would do more harm than good to speak. I shall say nothing.

OEDIPUS *angrily:* Nothing, you traitor? Will you say nothing? Will you stand by and see the city ruined by your stubbornness?

TIRESIAS: Whether I speak now, or leave without a word, nothing can prevent what's fated from happening!

OEDIPUS *exasperated:* It's precisely "what's fated" that I want you to tell me!

16

TIRESIAS: I shall say nothing. Rage as much as you like: you won't make me speak!

OEDIPUS *coldly:* My lord Tiresias, you've tried me too far now; I shall say what's in my mind. I believe *you* had a hand in this murder! I believe *you* planned the whole thing, and that you'd have struck the King down with your own hands, if you'd only had eyes to see him with!

TIRESIAS *grimly:* Is that what you think, King Oedipus? Very well, since you force me to speak, I shall say this much, at least: the curse you made just now was made against yourself. *Yourself,* Oedipus! You must obey your own proclamation! From this day onwards no one must speak to you or give you shelter—for the person responsible for the plague that's consuming Thebes, is *you yourself,* my lord!

OEDIPUS *furiously:* You *dare* say that to me? D'you think you can make a charge like that against the King, and not be punished?

TIRESIAS *quietly:* You won't punish me: what I'm saying is the truth.

OEDIPUS *icily:* Say it again, then! Say it once more—

TIRESIAS: Was once not enough? Must I repeat it?

OEDIPUS: Yes! I want there to be no doubt about it!

TIRESIAS *slowly and steadily:* You're searching for the murderer of Laius. Your search is over: for you are the murderer yourself. You killed him, no one else!

There is a brief pause, and then he adds:

Have you heard enough? Shall I say more?

OEDIPUS: You've already said enough to hang yourself! What more could you add?

TIRESIAS: Just this: the woman you married is nearer

related to you than you think! You committed another hideous crime by marrying her!

OEDIPUS: Am I to endure this any longer? D'you still expect not to be punished, after *this*?

TIRESIAS: Yes: for I believe that the truth is its own defence.

OEDIPUS *furiously*: It may be! It may be! But not for you! Nothing will save you now, you sightless, senseless, scheming slave!

But even under this tirade, the prophet remains calm.

TIRESIAS: I pity you: for one day men will taunt *you* with these very words!

OEDIPUS: Darkness is all you know, and you can do nothing to harm me—or anyone else with eyes to see!

TIRESIAS: No, I can't harm you: it wasn't your fate to fall at my hands. It's in Apollo's power to destroy you—and *he* won't fail you!

Suddenly in OEDIPUS' *mind a link suggests itself between* TIRESIAS, *Apollo, and the messenger the city sent to Delphi to ask the God for help.*

OEDIPUS *slowly*: Apollo . . . Delphi . . . Creon, my messenger!

He rounds on TIRESIAS.

Is *he* behind this plot?

TIRESIAS: The only person plotting against you is you yourself!

But now OEDIPUS *sees everything clearly, or so he thinks.*

OEDIPUS: Creon! I might have guessed it! The royal

wealth . . . the kingly crown . . . and a twisted envy,
plotting to destroy all its rivals . . . have these things
risen against me? Has Creon, my friend, my trusted
friend, whom I loved from the start, been planning all
this time to steal my throne—the throne the people gave
me as a freely-given gift? Has it come to this—that the
man I trusted most has turned against me, and has sent
this fraud to frighten me, this wizard here, this peddler of
empty tricks and shabby arguments, whose eyes can see
nothing but where his own advantage lies? Has he sunk
so low?

He turns mockingly to TIRESIAS.

You, prophet, tell me this: where did you pick up your
reputation for wise advice? When the Sphinx was here,
how did *you* help the city? What wise counsels had *you*
to offer then? A difficult adversary, not one for ordinary
men: it needed wisdom and great knowledge to guess her
riddle! And where were *you* then? What use were all
your birds and holy voices? None! It was left to me—to
me, the man you think so brainless!—to conquer her and
drive her away from Thebes! *I* had no birds to help me—
nothing but my own common sense—and yet I defeated
her! And that's the man you're trying to frighten, so as
to be first in the queue to lick King Creon's boots!
(*grimly*) Well, I warn you: this time you've gone too far,
you and your employer. The only thing saving you from
the punishment you deserve is your grey head—if you
were younger, I'd soon teach you where to look for
wisdom!

TIRESIAS *quietly, but grimly in his turn:* You're the King,
and can say what you like. But I demand one right: the

19

right to answer you. You called me a slave. I'm no man's slave, neither yours nor Creon's: I serve no one but Apollo. You called me a fraud, and taunted me with blindness. I tell you, although *you* can see as well as anyone else, you're as blind as I am: for you can't see the doom that's coming to engulf you, or who you are, or where you live, or who it is that shares your bed! Do you know who your parents are? Don't you realise how you've sinned against them, how their curse will drive you out of Thebes, as quickly as a conquering enemy's spears? Don't you see *that*, you who have eyes to see with? Stop my mouth if you like: have Creon silenced, too—but I swear to you that your death will be the most miserable any man has ever suffered!

OEDIPUS: Enough! I'll hear no more, you traitor! Leave me! Go back where you crawled from—and never dare come here again!

TIRESIAS: I'd never have come in the first place, if you hadn't sent for me!

OEDIPUS: And if I'd known the madness I was going to hear, I'd have thought twice before I did even that!

TIRESIAS: It may sound like madness to you—but your parents wouldn't call it that!

He turns to go.

OEDIPUS: Wait! What d'you mean, my parents?

TIRESIAS: This day has brought you into the world, and this day will see you leave it!

OEDIPUS: Must you always talk in riddles?

TIRESIAS: I thought you were famous for your skill at guessing them!

OEDIPUS: Mock it if you like—but that's what made me King!

TIRESIAS turns from him sadly.

TIRESIAS: I can do no more here . . .

OEDIPUS: Boy, take him home! We'll manage very well without him!

TIRESIAS: I shall go, then. But first I shall say what I came to say, whether you like it or not! For the last time, listen to me, Oedipus King of Thebes! The murderer of Laius, the criminal you're seeking with dreadful oaths and promises, the man all the hue and cry is after—is here, now, with me! A man everyone thought was a stranger to the city, but who'll soon find just how closely he belongs here. A rich man, with eyes to see—but when he knows the truth, a beggar, with a blind man's staff! Father of his children, and their brother; his mother's son and husband; heir to his father, and his murderer! That's what I came to say—see if you can solve *that* riddle! And when you've found the answer, then call me a liar and fraud if you like—and if you can!

He goes out, supported by his BOY. OEDIPUS gazes after him for a moment, then hurries into the palace.

CHORUS:
This was a fearful prophecy!
Tiresias is wise, wise beyond all other men—
And yet he is only mortal: he is not a God,
And he may still be wrong!
When the hideous Sphinx tormented the city,
It was Oedipus who helped us, who defeated her:
He saved the city then—will he destroy it now?
No feud has ever broken the friendship of the Kings
Of Thebes and Corinth: Polybus, Oedipus' royal father,
And Laius never quarrelled.

21

And yet this is the man the God has pointed at,
The man Apollo has denounced: now, like a bull
Walking the lonely hills, he is stalked by Death,
And the soft-footed Fates run swiftly after him.

*

SCENE THREE

Scene: the same. CREON *hurries in. in great agitation.*

CREON: Gentlemen of Thebes, is it true what they tell
me, that the King has made dreadful accusations against
me? What does he think I've done? What does he think
I've said? Does he believe I'd choose a time like this to
turn against him?

CHORUS: My lord—

CREON: How can I go on living after such a scandal?
How can I face my friends or my family, or lift up my
head in Thebes again?

CHORUS: My lord, what he said was said in anger—

CREON: Didn't he accuse me of bribing Tiresias to lie to
him?

CHORUS: My lord, why not question the King himself?
Here he is, just coming out of the palace.

OEDIPUS *comes in; when he sees* CREON, *he shouts
angrily:*

OEDIPUS: You, you traitor! Why have you come here?
You murdered the last King of Thebes, and you're trying to steal my throne—and still you dare to come before

me! What made you think this plot wouldn't be discovered? Or did you imagine I'd be too frightened to protect myself?

CREON: My lord, I—

OEDIPUS: How could you ever hope to succeed? No one supports you; no one wants you for their King—and I tell you, a man needs friends and influence to win a throne!

CREON: Oedipus, listen to me! At least hear what I have to say—after that, you can judge me any way you please!

OEDIPUS: Say what you like, you'll never convince me you're not my deadliest enemy!

CREON *desperately*: My lord—

OEDIPUS *ignoring him*: I suppose you think I'll let you go unpunished just because you're related to me! Well, I warn you: if that's what you expect, you're going to be disappointed!

CREON: But *how* have I harmed you? What have I done?

OEDIPUS: Didn't you persuade me to ask the advice of that wily fortune-teller?

CREON: Yes—and I still think I was right!

OEDIPUS: How long ago did Laius . . . disappear?

CREON: A long time—years ago.

OEDIPUS: And was this so-called "prophet" active then?

CREON: Yes, he was; and the people honoured him as highly as they do today!

OEDIPUS: And yet he told you nothing?

CREON: Nothing, as far as I know.

OEDIPUS *triumphantly*: I see! If he's so wise, why didn't

he give you a clue *then?* Why didn't he speak up when the first inquiry was held?

CREON: I don't know. I don't understand the ways of prophets—and I prefer to keep quiet about things I don't understand!

OEDIPUS: Well, perhaps you can answer me this: was there any good reason for him to accuse *me* of being the murderer—unless you'd planned it with him in advance?

CREON: If that's what he told you, I've nothing to say! But now you answer *me* a question, Oedipus!

OEDIPUS: What? I can only tell you that it wasn't me who murdered Laius!

CREON: But it was you who married my sister?

OEDIPUS: Of course: you know that as well as I do!

CREON: And you and she rule this country together?

OEDIPUS: We share the royal power between us, yes.

CREON: And am I not third in the Kingdom, after you two?

OEDIPUS: You are—and that's what makes your treachery so hard to bear!

CREON: But what makes you think I'd want to be a traitor? What makes you imagine I'd be eager to exchange a quiet life, with all the power I want, for the troubles and worries of being King? I'm satisfied with what I have already—I'm third in the land, and have almost as much authority as you yourself. I'm popular in the city; everyone is glad to see me; when people want an audience with you, they come and ask me to help them, because they know you always listen to my advice. D'you think I'd want to exchange this comfortable life for the difficult one of being King? Of course not—I'd be a fool if I did! And I'd be a bigger fool if I tried to make myself King by treachery! You can prove my loyalty, Oedipus: send messengers to Delphi, and ask whether the message the God gave me was the same as the one I brought back to you! And if you can find any plot between Tiresias and me, you may execute me in any way you please! But you won't find any plot, because there isn't one! You're accusing me of treason without any evidence—and it's as stupid and dangerous to think a loyal man a traitor as it is to think a traitor loyal! You'll find that out one day: for a traitor can be un-masked over-night, but it takes many years to prove the loyalty of one's friends!

CHORUS: He's spoken well, my lord: and it would be only prudent to listen to him. People who make hasty judgements are often sorry afterwards!

OEDIPUS: Don't be taken in! When a subtle man is plotting against you, you need to use subtlety as well, to defend yourself! If I did nothing now, I'd be playing right into his hands! No, I must deal with him myself! (*grimly*) And it won't be enough to banish him, either—the only way to make sure he's really safe is to have him executed!

CREON: But what have I done? What good will it do to execute me?

OEDIPUS: It's all you deserve, you traitor!

CREON: I tell you you're wrong!

OEDIPUS: Wrong or not, I am the King—

CREON: But not a just one!

CHORUS: Enough, enough, my lords! Here comes the Queen!

JOCASTA comes in from the palace. She is clearly very angry.

25

JOCASTA: Oedipus—and you too, Creon!—aren't you ashamed? Thebes is groaning with plague, and all you can do is stand here arguing! What's the matter? Have you no shame, quarrelling over some trivial matter, when the city desperately needs your help?

CREON: Some trivial matter? You don't know what you're saying, Jocasta! Your husband here—noble King Oedipus—is trying to make up his royal mind whether to banish me, or just have me executed!

OEDIPUS: Yes, Jocasta, that's the truth—for once! I found him plotting to overthrow me, and now he must pay the penalty for treason!

CREON: I tell you I'm innocent! I swear to you, by all the Gods, not one of your charges is justified! And I pray to be struck down, here and now, if that's not the truth!

JOCASTA: Oedipus, I beg you to listen to him! Believe his solemn oath, for all our sakes!

CHORUS: My lord, do as she advises—

OEDIPUS: Why? Why should I give way? You don't know what you're asking!

CHORUS: I'm asking you to believe him! You trusted him once—don't condemn him now without even listening to him!

OEDIPUS: You don't understand! If I let him go free, I'd be signing my own death-warrant! He's plotting to assassinate me!

CHORUS: My lord, I can't believe that's true! Please accept his word—the city's troubled enough, without a royal quarrel to add to our miseries! Please believe him! Listen to us now, and let him go!

There is a short pause.

OEDIPUS *reluctantly:* Very well. It'll probably mean my own death or banishment, but I'll do as you ask. For the city's sake, you understand, not his! As far as I'm concerned, he'll never be anything but a traitor!

CREON: I see you're the sort of man who never yields, who lets his anger drive out all his common sense—the sort of man who always ends up hurting himself more than anyone else!

OEDIPUS *angrily:* That's enough! I won't hear another word! Go now, quickly!

CREON: Yes, I'll go! But remember: no one else in Thebes thinks I'm guilty—only you!

He goes quickly out. OEDIPUS *walks up and down, trying to control his anger, while the* CHORUS *appeal to* JOCASTA:

CHORUS: My lady, couldn't you take the King inside, and try—

JOCASTA: First tell me how this quarrel started!

CHORUS: It started with a guess, a guess without any proof, that suddenly engulfed everyone, guilty and innocent alike!

JOCASTA: They each accused the other?

CHORUS: Yes.

JOCASTA: Of doing what?

CHORUS: Don't ask me to repeat it! Better forget the whole thing—for the city's sake!

OEDIPUS *suddenly rounds on them.*

OEDIPUS *bitterly:* You realise what you've done, you who were supposed to be so wise? You made me give way—and it'll probably be my downfall!

27

CHORUS: Sir, ask yourself one thing: would we betray you? Would we advise you to do anything we didn't believe was right? You saved Thebes once before—and we're looking to you now, as the one man who can save her again!

JOCASTA: My lord, they refuse to tell me what happened. Will *you*? Why have you suddenly turned against Creon?

OEDIPUS: I've "turned against him", as you put it, because I found him plotting against me!

JOCASTA: How? Was anything done or said openly?

OEDIPUS: He said that I was Laius' murderer!

JOCASTA *taken aback*: What? Had he any proof?

OEDIPUS: I don't know: he didn't make the accusation himself, but chose instead to shelter behind a sneaking prophet!

At this JOCASTA *laughs in sudden relief.*

JOCASTA: A prophet? So it was a prophet who made the accusation? Well, my lord, if *that's* all that's worrying you, you've nothing more to fear!

OEDIPUS: Why? What do you mean?

JOCASTA: There isn't one prophet whose word you can trust! They're nothing but frauds—all of them!

OEDIPUS: How do you know?

JOCASTA: I'll tell you. A prophet came to Laius, when he was still the King, and told him that his own son was fated to murder him. Notice that it was the *prophet* who told him, not the God himself! Laius and I were to have a son, and he was to kill his father—that's what was foretold.

OEDIPUS: Yes, and what happened?

JOCASTA: Isn't it obvious? *Was* he killed by his own

son? No! He was murdered, so far as we know, by travellers who attacked him at a crossroads, where three roads met—not by his own son at all! We *had* a son, it's true. But he was hardly three days old when we pinned his ankles together and left him to die, up in the mountains! Three days old! That proves how false oracles can be! Wait till the God speaks to you himself—don't take any notice of his priests!

But something in this speech has struck fear into OEDIPUS' *heart, and he answers her attempts at re-assurance with terror in his voice:*

OEDIPUS: Jocasta, there was something you said . . . something . . . I don't know, suddenly made me go cold with fear . . .

JOCASTA: What was it? You're quite pale!

OEDIPUS: You said, didn't you, that Laius . . . Laius was killed where three roads met?

JOCASTA: Three roads, yes: that was the story.

OEDIPUS *with sudden violence:* Where? Where? Where was the crossroads?

JOCASTA: Somewhere in Phocis, they said—where the road to Delphi joins the one from Daulia.

OEDIPUS: How long ago? Tell me quickly!

JOCASTA *mystified:* A short time before you became King of Thebes. Why?

OEDIPUS *as if crushed with terror:* My God! My God! What will you do to me?

JOCASTA: Oedipus, what's wrong? What's troubling you?

OEDIPUS *violently:* Don't ask! Don't make me tell you!

(in a whisper) What was he like . . . Laius? How old was he? What sort of man? . . .

J O C A S T A : Tall . . . hair beginning to turn grey . . . he looked rather like you, in fact!

O E D I P U S *still whispering, as though to himself:* Oh God! So I was the one I cursed just now!

J O C A S T A : What do you mean? What is it? You frighten me!

O E D I P U S : Could Tiresias see clearly after all? . . . *(suddenly, to* J O C A S T A*)* Tell me one thing more—was he alone? Or was he riding with a company of servants, as a King should?

J O C A S T A : There were five of them altogether, including a herald. There was just one carriage—the one Laius was riding in—

O E D I P U S : I guessed it! Jocasta, Jocasta, tell me this: who brought back news that the King was dead?

J O C A S T A : One of our servants—the only man who escaped the ambush.

O E D I P U S : And is he still here, still working in the palace?

J O C A S T A : No: when he came back to Thebes, and saw that you were King in Laius' place, he begged me to send him out into the country, as far from Thebes as possible. I saw no reason to refuse: he was a good, faithful servant, and—

O E D I P U S *desperately:* Could he be brought back? Can they bring him here, *immediately*?

J O C A S T A : I'll send for him at once. But what's the matter? What are you afraid of?

O E D I P U S : If what I'm afraid of is true, no one has more right to hear it than you! Listen, Jocasta: this is what's chilling my heart with fear . . .

With an effort he controls himself, and begins again, more calmly:

My father was Polybus, King of Corinth, and my mother's name was Merope. In my own city, no one was happier or prouder than Oedipus, the prince, their son . . . until, one day . . . it was very strange . . . someone who'd had too much to drink shouted at me that I wasn't the King's son at all, that Polybus wasn't my real father. I was deeply shaken, and the next morning I went to my father and mother and asked them for the truth. They were so upset by what the drunkard had said that I was reassured. But my certainty didn't last: the drunkard's words stayed there, nagging at my mind, until at last I decided to find out the truth once for all. Without telling my mother and father, I went to Delphi to ask the God whether I *was* Polybus' son or not. But Apollo didn't answer my question: instead he told me something so terrible that for days I didn't know what to do, or where to hide—

JOCASTA: Whatever did he tell you, to frighten you so badly?

OEDIPUS: He prophesied that one day I would murder my own father, and then marry my mother, and have children by her that men would shudder to see! I was horrified, and fled at once, trying to get as far from Corinth and my unhappy parents as I could. I decided never to return home, so that the prophecy could never be fulfilled. I travelled on and on, aimlessly, until eventually I came to Phocis—

JOCASTA: The country where Laius was murdered!

OEDIPUS: Yes! (*quietly*) And now every detail matters— I must try to leave nothing out . . . I came to a cross-

31

roads, a place where three roads met—and there I met a party of travellers: some men on horseback, led by a herald, and one single carriage, just as you describe it—

JOCASTA: And what happened?

OEDIPUS: The herald rode up to me and ordered me to let them pass—and the old man in the carriage shouted brusquely to me to get off the road. Then the driver of the carriage pushed me out of the way, and I lost my temper, and knocked him down . . . After that I started walking on my way, thinking that would be the end of the matter. But as I was passing the carriage window, the old man snatched the driver's whip, and slashed me across the face with it. He should never have done that: I was so angry that I hit him, hard, with the traveller's staff I was carrying, and he fell out of the carriage on to the road. After that they all attacked me, and I killed them all.

JOCASTA *horrified:* And you think it might have been—

OEDIPUS *grimly:* All I can say is, that if it was—if that old man was Laius, then there's no man more accursed than I! No one in Thebes may speak to me, or give me shelter; I must be driven out of the city—and I was the one who proclaimed it should be so! I killed the King of Thebes, and I've taken his palace, his kingdom, and his wife! Was I cursed the day I was born? First the dreadful prophecy that I would murder Polybus, my father—and now this! Where can I go, if I'm banished from Thebes? Not to Corinth—if I go there, the God has prophesied that I must kill my father and marry my mother! But I won't do it! I won't go back, cursed by such a fearful destiny!

CHORUS: My lord, this is a horrifying story. But there *is* one hope left: wait until you've seen the shepherd—

OEDIPUS: The shepherd, yes: he's my only hope!

JOCASTA: Hope? What do you mean?

OEDIPUS: If his story agrees with yours—if he says it was a *band* of robbers who killed the King, not one single man, then I'm saved! But if he says it *was* one man, travelling alone—

JOCASTA: But he won't! He didn't at the time, and he can't now! Everyone in the city heard him say it was a band of travellers—he can't tell a different story now: everyone would know he was lying!

OEDIPUS: Perhaps: you may be right! But I *must* see him, whatever his story, and find out the truth! He *must* be brought to Thebes!

JOCASTA: If you say so, my lord. Go inside, now, and send the palace guards to fetch him.

OEDIPUS goes into the palace, leaving JOCASTA standing lost in thought, while the CHORUS sing another ode. In their distress, feeling that no trust is left in the Gods, that they have abandoned men entirely, they sing in supplication to the King of the Gods, Zeus himself, begging him to come and help them.

CHORUS:

Zeus, lord of the world, arise!
For men are beginning to laugh at the Gods;
Apollo's prophecies are not fulfilled, and all
His shrines are tainted with dishonesty!

There is pride at work among men: foul pride,
Distended and swollen with unlawful gain—

33

Pride that laughs at the Gods, and scorns their laws;
Lord Zeus, arise and strike it down!

For the laws of the Gods are timeless:
They do not sleep, and they will never die;
Justice and piety are still at work in men,
And honouring Heaven is not yet made a crime!

If this is true: if the Gods are still at war
With human arrogance; if fools and criminals
May still expect to feel Heaven's anger—
Zeus, lord of the world, arise and help us now!

*

SCENE FOUR

Scene: the same, JOCASTA *is still standing where she was before.*

JOCASTA: Gentlemen, your prayer has moved me deeply: I shall go and sacrifice to the Gods once more. Oedipus is too upset to see things clearly: he'll believe anything he's told, provided it's frightening enough—and nothing I say seems to comfort him. So I shall go once more and pray to Apollo: he hasn't forsaken the city before, and I can't believe that he will now, even though I'll never trust his priests again! The Gods will help us, whatever their servants prophesy!

She is about to go, when an old man, the MESSEN- GER, *comes in. He looks round uncertainly, as though*

34

unsure of the way, and finally speaks respectfully to the CHORUS.

MESSENGER: My lords, can any of you direct me to the palace, or tell me where to find King Oedipus?

CHORUS: This is the palace, and you'll find the King inside. But this lady here is his wife, Jocasta, the Queen of Thebes.

The MESSENGER *kneels before* JOCASTA.

MESSENGER: My lady, may happiness always be yours, worthy wife of such a man !

JOCASTA: Sir, I thank you: you're welcome to Thebes. But tell me: what has brought you here? Have you some news for the King?

MESSENGER: Yes, my lady: good news, for him and everyone in the palace.

JOCASTA: What is it? Where are you from?

MESSENGER: From Corinth. What I have to say will delight you all—though it may upset you too.

JOCASTA: What can you say to delight us *and* upset us?

MESSENGER: This, my lady: the people of Corinth want to make Oedipus, your husband, their King—

JOCASTA: What? Isn't Polybus—

MESSENGER: Polybus is dead, my lady . . .

JOCASTA *with sudden excitement*: Dead? Oedipus' father, dead? (*to one of her* SERVANTS) Slave ! Go and ask your master to come out here, at once !

The SERVANT *goes into the palace.* JOCASTA *continues excitedly, as if to herself:*

That shows how much prophecies can be trusted ! Poly-

35

bus is dead—the man Oedipus was so terrified of murdering, *dead*! And not by his own son's hand after all!

OEDIPUS *comes out of the palace.*

OEDIPUS: My dearest Jocasta, why did you send for me?

JOCASTA: Listen to this man—and then see what you think of oracles!

OEDIPUS *to the* MESSENGER: What is it, my friend?

MESSENGER: My lord, this first of all: King Polybus is dead.

OEDIPUS *eagerly:* Dead? How? Was he murdered? Or did some sickness kill him?

MESSENGER: It doesn't take much to end an old man's life—

OEDIPUS: It *was* sickness, then?

MESSENGER: That and extreme old age.

OEDIPUS: You see, Jocasta! So much for Apollo's holy altars, and all the screaming birds and mystic voices that prophets rely on! I was to kill my father—that's what they foretold! And now—I never laid a finger on him, and he's dead! So much for oracles!

JOCASTA: You've nothing to fear from them again . . .

OEDIPUS *quietly:* Yes: there's still my mother . . . and the horrible prophecy that I must marry her . . .

JOCASTA: And you're still afraid of that? My lord Oedipus, there's no need! It's not prophecy that rules our lives, but chance, pure chance! We can't foretell anything that's going to happen—all we can do is live on, and wait and see what each day brings! You're afraid of marrying your own mother: but there's no need to be! Hundreds of men have dreamed of it before you, and none of them have ever done it! The only way to be happy is to ignore dreams like that: ignore them, and treat them with the contempt they deserve!

OEDIPUS *still unconvinced:* Words are no help . . . so long as she's alive, I'll never be able to shake off this fear . . .

MESSENGER: My lord, who is it you're afraid of?

OEDIPUS: Merope, sir, Polybus' Queen, my mother.

MESSENGER: What makes you so afraid of her?

OEDIPUS: An oracle, a dreadful oracle!

MESSENGER: What did it say? Can you tell it to a stranger?

OEDIPUS: Yes, I can tell you. Apollo told me, many years ago, that it was fated that I should marry my own mother, with my hands still red with my father's blood!

MESSENGER: And it was this that stopped you coming back to Corinth—you were afraid of fulfilling this terrible prophecy?

OEDIPUS: Yes, that's what I've been afraid of, ever since Apollo spoke.

MESSENGER: Well, my lord, your fears were groundless: for Polybus, King of Corinth, was no relation of yours whatsoever!

OEDIPUS *astonished:* What? Polybus was my father!

MESSENGER: No, sire, no more than I am!

OEDIPUS: What do you mean? I was honoured as his son!

MESSENGER: Yes, my lord: but I was the one who gave you to him!

OEDIPUS *surprised: Gave* me to him? Then I wasn't his son? But he loved me as a father!

MESSENGER: Until you came, he was childless: that was the reason.

OEDIPUS: And *you* gave me to him? But where did *you* find me?

MESSENGER: On the lower slopes of Mount Cithaeron.

OEDIPUS: What brought you there?

MESSENGER: I was a shepherd, sir, tending sheep on the mountainside. And if I hadn't come along when I did, you'd never have survived—I rescued you!

OEDIPUS: What from? Was anything the matter with me?

MESSENGER: Your weak ankles, my lord, should answer that question!

OEDIPUS: My ankles! They've always been weak—but how did *you* know about them?

MESSENGER: They were pinned together when you came to me, and I released them!

OEDIPUS: Pinned together? Yes, I still have the scars! But who pinned them—my mother, or my father? Can you tell me that?

MESSENGER: No, my lord: only the man who gave you to me could answer that!

OEDIPUS: I thought you said you found me yourself!

MESSENGER: No, sire: I met another shepherd on Cithaeron, and he gave you to me.

OEDIPUS *eagerly:* Who was he? Can you remember his name?

MESSENGER: No—but they said he was a servant of King Laius.

OEDIPUS *is too intrigued by what the* MESSENGER *is telling him to notice how, as the tale unfolds,* JOCASTA *has been stricken with mounting horror.*

OEDIPUS: A servant of Laius? Is he still alive? Could I speak with him?

MESSENGER: These gentlemen could tell you that better than I.

OEDIPUS *to the* CHORUS: Sirs, have any of you seen the man he means—in the fields, perhaps, or here in the city? Can any of you tell me who he is?

CHORUS: My lord, I think it might well be the shepherd you sent for just now, the man who was with Laius when he was murdered. But only the Queen could tell you for certain.

OEDIPUS: Can you, Jocasta? Is it the same man?

JOCASTA *very agitatedly:* My lord, forget him! Pay no attention to them! Forget what's been said! It's all in the past now, past and forgotten!

OEDIPUS: What do you mean? I'm coming close at last to discovering who my parents were—why are you trying to stop me?

JOCASTA: Oedipus, I beg you: go no further! It would break my heart!

OEDIPUS *surprised, and a little annoyed:* What are you afraid of? Even if my mother was the most miserable of slaves, it won't affect *you*!

JOCASTA *pleadingly:* Please, Oedipus—*please*!—inquire no further!

OEDIPUS: I must, until I find out the truth!

JOCASTA: It's for your own good!

OEDIPUS: I'm tired of doing things 'for my own good'! I want to know the truth!

JOCASTA *despairingly:* Oedipus, I beg you, stop now! You're doomed, and you don't realise it!

OEDIPUS: Doomed? (*mockingly, to the* CHORUS) She's afraid I'm the son of a slave! But I don't care who my mother was! Guards! Go and fetch the shepherd!

JOCASTA: Oedipus, Oedipus, you don't know what you're doing! You're lost, lost for ever—listen to me now, for you never will again!

She hurries into the palace.

CHORUS: She's gone, my lord—and in great distress. What can her last words have meant? I didn't like the sound of them!

OEDIPUS: It doesn't matter now! However humble their birth, I *must* find out who my parents were! Jocasta's a queen, a great lady, and she's ashamed to think she may have married the son of a slave—but I'*m* not ashamed, whoever my mother was! I *must* find out the truth! I *must* know, beyond all question, who and what I am!

At this point, to emphasise the heightening tension of the situation, the CHORUS sing a brief ode.

CHORUS:

Cithaeron, tomorrow you shall fill our song:
Tomorrow Thebes will be dancing in your honour!
For Oedipus is no one's son but yours:
You are his father, his mother, and his nurse—
On your fair slopes the King of Thebes was born!

Who was your mother, Oedipus? A mountain-nymph,
Immortal bride of Pan who walks the hills?
Apollo loves our rolling meadowland—was he
Your father? Or was it Bacchus, who prefers to roam
The grassy haunts of the Muses, far-famed Helicon?

OEDIPUS, who has been looking anxiously off-stage, now turns to them.

OEDIPUS: Gentlemen, I've never seen the shepherd before; but it seems to me that this is him coming now! He's an old man—about the same age as the Corinthian here—and it's my guards who're bringing him in. You know him: tell me, is it the same man?

CHORUS: Yes, my lord, it is: one of Laius' most faithful servants.

OEDIPUS *to the* MESSENGER: Was this the man you meant, sir?

MESSENGER: Yes, my lord.

The GUARDS *bring in an old* SHEPHERD, *who kneels before* OEDIPUS.

OEDIPUS: Stand up, shepherd, and answer these questions as truly as you can. You were one of Laius' servants, were you not?

SHEPHERD: Yes, sir, one of his shepherds.

OEDIPUS: Where?

SHEPHERD: On Mount Cithaeron mostly, or in the countryside round about.

OEDIPUS: And this man here: have you ever seen him before?

The SHEPHERD *looks closely at the* MESSENGER, *then speaks doubtfully.*

SHEPHERD: No, my lord . . . not that I can remember . . .

MESSENGER: It's hardly surprising: it was a very long time ago. But I'll try and jog his memory. Three summers we spent together on Cithaeron: he had two flocks of sheep, and I had one. Every winter we separated: I drove my sheep back to Corinth, and he took his to Laius' sheep-folds, here in Thebes. (*to the* SHEPHERD) Isn't that right?

SHEPHERD *still doubtfully:* Yes . . . yes . . . I think so . . . it was a long time ago . . . I think I remember you now . . .

MESSENGER: And do you also remember giving me a child you'd found on the mountain, and asking me to bring it up as my own son?

SHEPHERD *startled:* A child? What do you mean? Why do you ask me that?

MESSENGER: Because this man here, the King himself, is that same child, grown-up now!

SHEPHERD *violently:* Be quiet, damn you! It's a pack of lies—lies, do you hear?

OEDIPUS: Sir, sir, control yourself! *You* seem to be the one that's lying, not him!

SHEPHERD: Lying, my lord?

OEDIPUS: Do you deny his story about the child?

SHEPHERD: He doesn't know what he's saying!

OEDIPUS: You'd better tell me the truth: if you won't, there are ways of making you talk—

SHEPHERD *terrified:* No sire, no, I beg you! I'm an old man, too old for torture!

OEDIPUS: Guards! Take him away!

SHEPHERD *almost babbling with terror:* Why, my lord? I'm innocent! I've done nothing!

OEDIPUS: Did you or did you not give him that child?

SHEPHERD *desperately:* Yes, yes, I admit it! I wish I'd died before I ever set eyes on him!

OEDIPUS: So he *did* get it from you? And where did *you* get it from? Was it your own son?

SHEPHERD: No, no!

OEDIPUS: Well, who gave it to you?

The SHEPHERD *looks round in terror, but is silent.* Guards!

SHEPHERD *reluctantly:* I got it from . . . someone else!

OEDIPUS: Who?

SHEPHERD *wildly:* Please, my lord, don't question me any more !

OEDIPUS *grimly:* I don't want to have to ask you again—

SHEPHERD: My lord, I daren't . . .

OEDIPUS *relentlessly:* Tell me ! Whose child was it?

SHEPHERD *with extreme reluctance:* It was a child of . . . of Laius' house !

OEDIPUS: Laius' house? Who was its father? One of his slaves?—or someone else?

SHEPHERD: My lord, I can't tell you ! I'm doomed if I speak now !

OEDIPUS *grimly; he begins to suspect the truth:* And so am I, I think ! But none the less, you must speak ! *Whose child was it?*

SHEPHERD: They said . . . they said it was the King's own son ! My lord, I can't tell you any more . . . the Queen—

OEDIPUS *sharply:* The Queen? Did *she* give him to you?

The SHEPHERD *is silent.*

Speak, man !

The SHEPHERD *remains silent, and* OEDIPUS *signs to the* GUARDS.

SHEPHERD *in an anguished voice:* Yes, yes, my lord !

OEDIPUS: Why? What for?

SHEPHERD: To kill, sire !

OEDIPUS: Her own son?

SHEPHERD: There was some terrible prophecy—

OEDIPUS: Yes?

SHEPHERD: About him . . . about him killing his own father . . .

OEDIPUS: And why didn't you obey orders? Why didn't

43

you kill the child at once? What made you give it to *him*?

SHEPHERD: I . . . I couldn't kill him! He was only a baby, sir, a harmless little baby . . . I hadn't the heart . . . I thought . . . I thought if I sent him out of the country somewhere, he'd be safe . . . as far away as possible . . . this fellow took him to Corinth! Oh, I wish I'd never set eyes on him!

Suddenly he breaks off, and looks straight at OEDIPUS.

My lord, I pity you! If you were that same child, I pity you! The Gods have cursed you utterly!

OEDIPUS: Enough, enough! It's clear to me at last! I know my father's name, and who I married! I know whose blood I shed, and who it was who bore my children! Oh Zeus, can I ever look on the light of day again? I know who I am at last—and is there room on earth for such a man as I?

He stumbles into the palace. The GUARDS *escort the* MESSENGER *and the* SHEPHERD *from the stage, while the* CHORUS *softly begin a mourning song.*

CHORUS:

Can any man claim true happiness is his?
Will he not soon awake, to a grey dawn, showing
How all his joy was but an empty dream?
Are all men not like Oedipus?

Oedipus, the King!—who broke the power
Of the subtle Sphinx, and proved himself
A lighthouse in the storm of Thebes' dark agony—
Was ever any man more fortunate?

And has any man fallen from a higher peak?
Has anyone ever tasted more unhappiness?

His wife his mother, his brothers his own sons—
Can anyone claim more bitter grief?
Oedipus, the King!—once great, now doomed:
Time found him out, and brought him low—
Weep, then, for Oedipus, Thebes' brightest sun,
Whose dawn is now drowned in darkest night!

*

SCENE FIVE

As the CHORUS *finish their song, a* SERVANT
hurries out of the palace.

SERVANT: Rulers of Thebes, I've terrible news to bring
you! Terrible to hear, terrible to see, and terrible to
report!

CHORUS: What has happened?

SERVANT: A pollution so horrible, that all the rivers of
Thebes will never wash it clean!

CHORUS: Could anything be worse than what we know
already?

SERVANT: Yes, this! Jocasta the Queen is dead!

CHORUS: Dead? How?

SERVANT: By her own hand! I'll never forget the sight!

CHORUS: But how did it happen?

SERVANT: You saw her rushing into the palace just now?

CHORUS: When she hurried away in such deep distress?

SERVANT: Yes. She went into her own room, and slammed
the doors and locked them behind her. All we could hear

45

from inside was the sound of hopeless, bitter sobbing. She kept calling for Laius, and cursing their son, the son who killed his father, and then married her—his mother!—and gave her children of his own. Then suddenly everything went deathly quiet, and we feared the worst. We were just about to break down the doors when Oedipus burst in, shouting and screaming like a madman . . . He rushed round the room like a caged animal, coming up to each one of us in turn and begging us to give him a sword. "Where is she?" he kept screaming. "Where's my wife, no wife, the woman who's both my and my children's mother? Tell me where she is!" He was like a madman—it was horrible to hear! . . . None of us spoke: it must have been some God that whispered to him where she was. For suddenly he rushed up to the doors of her bedroom, kicked them and hammered on them with his fists, trying to break them down . . At last the lock gave way, and he burst in—and there she was, dangling from a noose in the middle of the room. With a terrible cry the King went up to her, untied her, and laid her gently on the floor. Then—

He pauses.

CHORUS: What happened?

SERVANT: It was horrible! There were some golden pins fastening her dress at the shoulder: the King snatched them, and stabbed them furiously into his own eyes, with all his strength, shouting: "I've seen enough! I'll never look on her again! Darkness! Darkness for ever more! That's all I'll look on now! I'll never again see the wife it was a crime to marry, the children who should never have been born! Darkness! Night and darkness—that's all I'll ever see!" With every word he stabbed the pins

46

into his eyes afresh; blood was pouring down his cheeks
—it was horrible! To think that happiness like theirs
should come to this: death and weeping, and hopeless,
crushing misery!

CHORUS: Where is he now?

SERVANT: Inside, shouting to them to open the palace
doors, and show him to the people: the man who murdered his father and married his mother; the man who
cursed himself, and outlawed himself from his own city!

Suddenly they hear the sound of bolts being drawn.

But see for yourself: they're opening the palace doors.

The great doors are slowly opened wide, and
OEDIPUS, *blind, comes out on to the marble steps.*

OEDIPUS *humbly, all his pride now gone:*
>   Can any of you tell me
>   Where I am? Or what has happened?
>   What have the Gods done to me?

CHORUS:
>   Something too frightful to see or hear.

OEDIPUS:
>   Everything about me is dark:
>   I am surrounded by pitchblack night,
>   With no hope of dawn to brighten it.

CHORUS:
>   My lord, you have suffered grievously—

OEDIPUS *turns gropingly towards the sound.*

OEDIPUS:
>   Who is that? My counsellor?
>   My truest friend, staying to comfort me?

I cannot see you: I can only hear
Your voice. Is it you, my friend?

CHORUS:

My lord,
How could you bear to do it? Your own eyes!
How could you bear to blind them?

OEDIPUS:

It was the Gods
Who guided me: it was Apollo who brought
This suffering upon me, who made me lift
My hands against myself. And yet, what use
Would eyes be to me now? All that is left
To see is shame and hideous guilt!

CHORUS *quietly:*

You are right, sire.

OEDIPUS:

I'd never have had the right
To look on what was beautiful, or hear
What was sweet to hear, again. No! It is finished:
You must take me away, my friend, lead me far
From Thebes: I swore an oath, and I must obey!

CHORUS:

I pity you: I wish you had never learned
How deeply you had sinned, how great your guilt.

OEDIPUS *with sudden vehemence:*

Damn him! Damn the man who found me,
A helpless child on the mountainside,
The man who freed me, gave me life,
And left me to be the doom of those I loved!

CHORUS:

Would it had not been so!

OEDIPUS:

> Father-slayer, mother's bridegroom I am called;
> Godless, accursed, brother of my sons—
>
> Is there any dreadful name I have not earned?

CHORUS:

> And yet, my lord, was any of your crimes
> Great enough for such a fearful punishment?

OEDIPUS:

> Yes! No other would have been enough! How could
> I have looked on my dear dead father, or on her,
> My unhappy mother? Death itself would have been
> Too light a punishment for what I did to them!
> And my children—how could I have looked on them,
> Born of my own mother, who was also my wife?
> And how could I ever have seen fair Thebes again?
> How could I have looked on her towers, her shrines,
> Her busy market-place? I cursed myself
> Unwittingly, Thebes' ruler, and her son:
> I ordered my own banishment—I forbade
> All men to shelter Laius' murderer!
> No! Even blindness is not enough! I would
> Dam up my ears, destroy my body utterly,
> Until no senses were left to me: for pain
> And misery are all I have left to feel!
> Cithaeron, why did you shelter me? Why
> Did you not let me die at once, instead
> Of saving me, to find out whose son I was?
> Corinth, and Polybus whom I called my father,
> Did you not guess how accursed a man he was,
> The fair young prince you cherished as your own?
> Did you not see how shamefully my life
> Was doomed to end? At a deserted crossroads,

49

Shaded on each side by silent, watchful trees,
Whose roots I spattered with my father's blood!
Why did I not die there? Why did I come
To Thebes, and a hideous, unholy marriage-bed?
Fathers, brothers, sons—all born from one
Unhappy mother-wife, a sight so gross,
So foul, that men must shrink to look on it!
Can you not see how blindness is best for me?
Will you not kill me now, or bury me,
Or sink me in the sea's green depths? My lords,
If you can bear to touch me, cast me out
Of Thebes—for God's sweet sake, cast me out now!

CHORUS: Oedipus, it's not for us to decide your fate. By your abdication—since your sons are still under age—Creon is now King of Thebes.

OEDIPUS: Creon! What can I say to him? How can I apologise for the accusations I made against him?

There is a fanfare in the distance.

CHORUS: My lord, you must try: for he is coming now.

CREON *comes in, followed by servants leading* ANTIGONE *and* ISMENE, *the two younger children of* OEDIPUS.

CREON: Oedipus, I haven't come to laugh at you, or reproach you for what you said the last time we met. No: we must mourn this tragedy together—but privately, not here, before the eyes of all the people. Will you come inside, with me?

OEDIPUS *kneels to him, humbly.*

OEDIPUS: My lord, I must thank you for speaking so kindly: it was more than I deserved. May I make one request—one to your advantage to grant as well as mine to ask?

CREON: What is it, that you beg so humbly?

OEDIPUS: Cast me out of Thebes! Banish me, where no one will ever see me again!

CREON: My lord, your fate isn't mine to decide: we must wait for Apollo's instructions.

OEDIPUS: Apollo? Hasn't he spoken already? Didn't he say that Laius' murderer was to be driven from the city? Isn't that what he commanded?

CREON: He did, yes—but now we know *who* the murderer was, we must ask for clearer instructions.

OEDIPUS: I understand; and I bow to your command. But Jocasta—what's to become of her? Creon, will you promise me this: will you bury her as a Queen deserves? She *was* your own sister! All I ask for myself is to be sent away from the city—send me into the mountains, to die there! Yes, to Cithaeron, the place my parents chose for my death! Send me there, and I will carry out their wishes!

CREON *sadly:* If that is what you want, I must agree.

OEDIPUS: Just one thing more—

CREON: What?

OEDIPUS: My children: not the boys . . . they can fend for themselves . . . but the two girls, Antigone and Ismene—will you look after them, bring them up for me? You're all they have left—

CREON *gently:* I'll take care of them.

The little girls, not really understanding what is happening, begin to cry bitterly at the thought of being parted from their father.

OEDIPUS: What's that? Are they here? May I speak to

51

them . . . touch them . . . say goodbye to them for the
last time?

CREON: Yes, they're here. I had them brought in, knowing
how you love them still.

OEDIPUS: May Heaven reward you for your kindness—
and make your life an easier one than mine!

He turns to the children.

My little ones, where are you? Come here to me,
And let me touch you: let your brother's hands
Caress you for the last time! (*gently*) These are the hands
That stole your father's eyesight: he can't see you,
My darlings—he can only share your weeping!

*He continues with some bitterness, more to himself
than to the children:*

What sort of life will yours be now? What will you do
On the city's feast-days—how will you be able
To endure the sight of others' happiness?
And when you reach the age for marriage, who
Will dare to take you, cursed as you are
With the terrible name of Oedipus, your father?
Are you not damned for ever? Your father killed
His own father; his wife—his mother!—was your
Sad mother too! Is that not shame enough?
Who will ignore this curse, and marry you?
No one, my daughters: you will die unwed—
So prophesies the father who brought his curse
Upon you. Creon, I commend them to you:
Their parents are dead or doomed, and you are all
They have—be kind to them, my lord! Don't let
Them wander to a dark death in friendless misery!
Take pity on them: they have no one else!

CREON: I will.

OEDIPUS: My friend, I thank you. Let me shake
  Your hand!

He turns back to the children.

  I must leave you now, my daughters.
  When you're older, you'll understand what the Gods
  Have done to me: pray now—as I do—that you
  May live more happily than your father did!

*CREON signs to the servants, who lead the children
gently into the palace.*

CREON: Will you go in now, my lord?

OEDIPUS: Yes: I must—
  And yet it is a bitter ending.

CREON: Bitter,
  But fated from the start. Will you go in?

*He leads OEDIPUS into the palace. The stage is now
empty of everyone except the CHORUS.*

CHORUS:
  People of Thebes, behold Oedipus the King:
  He solved the Sphinx's riddle, and ruled this land
  In might and honour; all men envied him
  His wealth and happiness. Now all his might
  Is gone, drowned in a stormy sea of trouble.
  Behold him now, and learn from his sad fate:
  A man may live in peace and honour all
  His life—but may not claim true happiness,
  Until, untroubled to the last, he sleeps,
  Beyond the reach of care, in his own quiet grave.

*

2

ANTIGONE

NOTE

After the terrible end of Oedipus' reign his brother-in-law Creon became governor of Thebes, ruling as regent until Eteocles and Polynices, Oedipus' sons, the rightful heirs, should come of age. Under his government the city prospered once again; and as his children and those of Oedipus grew up, his younger son, Haemon, forgetting the curse Oedipus had placed upon his daughters, fell in love with the elder of them, Antigone, and planned to marry her, believing it to be a sign that Apollo's curse had worked itself out, and that Oedipus' descendants, at least, were to be allowed to live normal, happy lives.

But they rejoiced too soon: the curse on the house of Labdacus was not yet extinct. As Oedipus' sons grew to manhood, a terrible quarrel broke out between them, as to which of them should become King of Thebes. Eteocles was the elder, and the throne was his by right; but his brother Polynices felt that he, too, had a right to rule. To enforce his claim he left the city, and returned with an army from the hostile state of Argos, intending to besiege and conquer Thebes, and win the throne by force of arms.

Eteocles, however, led the Theban champions so well that the besieging army was for a long time unable to capture the city. The siege dragged on and on, until at last it was decided to end it by a series of single combats, one champion from Polynices' force meeting one from Thebes. Seven such contests were held, one outside each of the seven gates of the city. In the last of them the two brothers fought, the rebel and the defender of the city. For a whole day they struggled, watched by anxious crowds on the city wall—

crowds including their sisters, Antigone and Ismene, their cousin, the young man Haemon, and their uncle Creon, who would become King, instead of regent, if neither of them survived.

And that, in fact, is how the contest ended: neither side won; each prince killed the other, and with Polynices' death his army lost heart and withdrew, leaving the city unsure whether to dance with joy at having been saved from the invader, or to go into deepest mourning for the two dead princes.

It is at this point that the play of ANTIGONE begins. . . .

ANTIGONE

Characters:

CREON, *the King of Thebes*
EURYDICE, *his wife, the Queen*
HAEMON, *his son*
ANTIGONE ⎫
ISMENE   ⎬ *his nieces*
TIRESIAS, *the blind prophet*
MESSENGER
GUARD

CHORUS of *Theban elders*

Guards, servants, boy leading Tiresias, etc.

ANTIGONE

SCENE ONE

*The scene is an open space before the palace of Creon,
King of Thebes. It is the day after the great battle, in
which Eteocles, leader of the Theban champions, and his
rebel brother, Polynices, killed each other in single com-
bat. The elder sister of the two dead princes,* ANTIGONE,
is waiting impatiently for her sister ISMENE. *When she
appears,* ANTIGONE *hurries up to her in some agitation.*

ANTIGONE: Oh, Ismene, Ismene, are we to be spared no
punishment from Heaven? Is there any pain or humilia-
tion left for us to suffer? Have you heard Creon's latest
proclamation—the one echoing round the city even now?
Has no one told you how they're treating our brothers
like enemies?

ISMENE: Our brothers? No: I've heard no news of them
since that terrible moment when they died together—
I've heard nothing since the Argive army left last night.

ANTIGONE: I thought not: that's why I sent for you out
here, where no one can overhear us.

ISMENE: But what is it? What are you hiding from me?

ANTIGONE: You don't know how Creon is treating our
brothers, honouring one and disgracing the other? How
he's burying Eteocles with all the pomp and honour the
Dead deserve, but is leaving Polynices' corpse unwashed,
unburied, for vultures to feed on?

ISMENE *aghast:* What?

ANTIGONE: Yes, that's the news! That's what our noble

lord, great Creon, has proclaimed—proclaimed to dishonour you and me, not just our brothers! And he's coming here to proclaim it again, so that no one can plead ignorance, and to make it clear that it's no empty threat —the penalty for disobedience is death by public stoning! *That's* my news! *That's* what I had to tell you!

She pauses, expecting some horrified reaction from her sister. But ISMENE *remains silent, and she adds sharply:*

Well, what do you say now? Will you choose nobly, choose like a true King's daughter, or not?

ISMENE: Choose? What do you mean? What could I do or say that would be any use?

ANTIGONE: Will you help me?

ISMENE: Help you what?

ANTIGONE: Help me bury[1] the corpse!

ISMENE *horrified:* Bury Polynices! . . . when we are all forbidden—

ANTIGONE: Yes, bury him! Bury my brother—and yours too, for all you may wish he wasn't! I at least shan't betray him!

ISMENE: It would be madness! Against Creon's orders, to bury—

ANTIGONE: This concerns only my brothers and me— it's nothing to do with Creon!

ISMENE: Oh, Antigone, think!

ANTIGONE: Think? Think what?

---

[1] The Greeks believed that anyone left unburied was condemned to eternal misery. To avoid this fate, it was sufficient to scatter a handful of dust over the dead man, while praying that he might find happiness among the Dead.

ISMENE: Think of our father's death! Think of him tearing out his own eyes in agony for his crimes, Oedipus who married his mother! Think of her, too, his mother-wife, choking to death in a twisted noose! Think of our unhappy brothers, murdering each other on a single day! Now we alone are left, the two of us—and think how *we* shall suffer, if we disobey King Creon's orders!

ANTIGONE: But—

ISMENE: Remember we're only women, not made to fight with men!

ANTIGONE: Ismene, listen to me—

ISMENE: Our father was a King: let our royal blood teach us to bear this—and worse than this—bravely! I pray that my dear dead brother will forgive me, but I can't disobey Creon! It would be madness!

ANTIGONE *coldly:* Very well. I shan't ask you again. Even if you begged to help me now, I wouldn't accept! You may do as you please: but I am going to bury him! After that, death will be sweet—

ISMENE *terrified:* Antigone!

ANTIGONE: I shall do what I must, and lie beside my own dear brother, friend with friend. We've only a moment to please the living, but all eternity to please the Dead! There's no going back. You may scorn the Gods if you like!

ISMENE: I'm not scorning the Gods—but I can't defy the King!

ANTIGONE: Do as you please: I at least shall give my brother a proper burial!

ISMENE: I'm afraid for you—

ANTIGONE: Don't worry about me: think about yourself!

62

ISMENE, *seeing that it is impossible to dissuade her, now tries a different approach:*

ISMENE: Very well, do it if you must. But keep it secret! Tell no one what you've done—I'll keep silent too!

ANTIGONE: Keep silent? No! Cry it aloud to everyone, or I'll hate you more than ever! The whole city must know what I've done!

ISMENE: I'm frightened, Antigone . . .

ANTIGONE: I'm not—because I'm doing what I know is right!

ISMENE: If you can—if you have the strength!

ANTIGONE: Lack of strength will not prevent me.

ISMENE: It's madness! Why must you try to do the impossible?

ANTIGONE: Impossible? Don't use words like that, or the Dead will begin to hate you too! "Madness" you call it—but let me follow it out to the end! At least I shall earn a noble death!

She hurries out, leaving ISMENE *to cry after her:*

ISMENE: Go on, then! But remember: whatever you do, there are those of us who love you still!

She goes into the palace. The CHORUS *now enter the dancing-place in procession, singing an ode praising Zeus for Eteocles' victory over the invading Argives.*

CHORUS:
We greet you, eye of the golden morning,
Protectress of this fair city, the dawn
Whose brightness broke the Argives' might
And sent them whimpering home.

Polynices led them, proud Polynices,
Hovering, dark as an eagle, over us:
The plain was filled with his nodding plumes,
And bristled with thirsty Argive spears.

Then, like an eagle, he swooped upon us,
Soaring down on his snow-white wings;
Swooped on our crown of seven gates,
To gorge himself on our Theban blood.

But Zeus saw: Zeus heard his boasting,
And watched his glittering army flood the plain.
Zeus saw;
And sent him crashing down.

Down he fell, and the earth echoed;
Down in battle fell his champions:
This was the fruit of his proud boasting;
This was his anger's swift reward.

Seven champions at Thebes' seven gates
Offered up the arms of their enemies
As a thank-offering to almighty Zeus.

And these two, sons of one father,
Sons of one unhappy mother, fell
Together, victims of each other's fate.

This was our victory: this is the theme
Of our song in the temples of the Gods,
Dancing till the new dawn comes,
In honour of Zeus, and the eagle's fall.

*

SCENE TWO

Scene: the same. As the C H O R U S finish their song, a fanfare of trumpets is heard in the distance.

C H O R U S : Here comes Creon, Menoiceus' son. Perhaps he's coming to tell us the news he promised us : dreadful news indeed, to judge from the haste with which he sent for us.

Another fanfare sounds from near at hand, and C R E O N comes in.

C R E O N : Gentlemen, I summoned you here, now that the Gods have brought us safely through the war, to ask for your support. I know how loyal you were to the old King, Laius, and to his son, Oedipus, who saved us from the Sphinx. I know how, when Oedipus died, you transferred your loyalty to his sons Eteocles and Polynices. But now both these princes are dead, too, each by the other's hand. Because I'm their nearest male relative (and Antigone and Ismene, their sisters, being women, cannot rule), the supreme power passes to me, and I inherit the throne by right of blood.

But I'm not asking for your loyalty immediately. For I know a man must be tried in office before his ways are made clear, and his views, principles and intentions become obvious.

There *is* one thing, however, that I'd like to state clearly to you now : I've no time for any ruler who's afraid to pass an essential law because it will make him unpopular. There's only one thing worse, in my opinion : for a man to put loyalty to his friends before his country. I hope I can say truthfully that I'd avoid both these faults: I'd tell you at once of any trouble approaching Thebes, and I'd never choose one of her enemies as my friend. That's how I feel, and that's how I mean to rule.

It's because of this that I make you the following proclamation: Eteocles, son of Oedipus, prince of the royal house of Thebes, who died honourably, fighting for his native land, is to be buried with all the pomp and honour that we owe the Dead. But his brother Polynices—who left Thebes as a fugitive, and came back with an army to raze it to the ground and slaughter and enslave its people—he is to be left to rot, a naked corpse for dogs and birds of prey to tear at. No one is to bury him or mourn for him. That's my decree—for I'll never allow any faithful soldier of mine to share honours with a common criminal!

CHORUS: If this is your will, my lord, no one will dare to disobey.

CREON: It's your duty to make sure of that!

CHORUS: You mean, guard the corpse? Couldn't a younger man—

CREON: There are guards posted already.

CHORUS: What must *we* do, then?

CREON: See that no one disobeys: "discourage" them!

CHORUS: No one would dare! With death the penalty—

CREON *grimly:* Death *is* the penalty! But you can never tell what bribery will make men do!

He is about to go, when the GUARD *comes in slowly. He speaks hesitantly, as though afraid of being punished.*

GUARD: My lord . . .

CREON: Yes, what is it?

GUARD: Sir, I wouldn't like you to think . . . er . . . that is . . .

He hesitates.

CREON *a little impatiently*: Well, come on! What d'you want?

GUARD: Well, it's not because I . . . you see . . .

CREON: Get on with it!

GUARD *plucking up all his courage*: My lord, it's not hurrying that's made me out of breath: don't think that! No—I spent most of the journey wondering whether it wouldn't be better to turn back! "You fool!" I said to myself, "You'll be sorry if you do go to him, I can tell you!" Then I thought: "No, no: no use not going! Suppose he heard about it from someone else? Then you'd cop it!"

CREON: What are you talking about?

GUARD: That's what made the journey so long, all this to-ing and fro-ing . . . Anyway, at last I decided it was best to come after all, and tell you—though it's not much to tell, at that!

CREON: But what *is* it?

GUARD: You see, I decided that whatever came to me was fated to happen in any case, and nothing I could do would prevent it!

CREON: Prevent *what*?

GUARD: Let me make this clear first of all: it was nothing to do with me! I didn't do it, and I didn't see who did! It would be wrong for me to get into trouble unjustly!

CREON: You'll get into trouble all right, if you don't hurry up and come to the point!

GUARD: It's just that I don't want you to think—

CREON *exasperated:* For goodness' sake say what you came to say, and then clear off!

GUARD *gloomily:* All right, I'll tell you. It's the corpse: someone's gone and buried it!

CREON *in great surprise:* What?

GUARD: Someone's covered it with dust, and made the usual offerings.

CREON: Who can have dared—

GUARD: There's no way of telling: there weren't any spademarks round about, or signs that a pickaxe had been used. The ground's hard, you see, hard and dry, and you don't leave footprints, or even wheelmarks in it—

CREON: So there's no clue?

GUARD: No, none at all.

CREON: Who discovered what had happened?

GUARD: We didn't find out until the sentry took up his post this morning. Then we discovered it: there he was, hidden—not buried proper, you understand, just covered lightly with earth, as though someone had done it to avoid pollution!

CREON: Could it have been an animal?

GUARD: There were no signs that anything had been near—nothing had picked at the corpse, at any rate! You should have heard the fuss there was when we found him! Guard accusing guard of doing it, everyone shouting at everyone else: I tell you, we were each of us ready to walk through fire, or pick up red-hot iron, and swear by all the Gods we'd neither done it nor been in the know about it! It might have ended in a free-for-all—but someone suddenly said something that shut us all up quick: scared the living daylights out of us—

68

CREON: What was that?

GUARD *uncomfortably*: My lord, I hardly like to say . . .

CREON: Come on, man! What was it?

GUARD *reluctantly*: Well, my lord, he pointed out that . . . that someone would have to come and tell *you* what had happened!

CREON: *What?*

GUARD: There was no sense in hiding it! Well, in the end we drew lots who was to be the unlucky one—begging your pardon, sir!—and of course it had to be me! And here I am! Believe me, I wanted to tell you as little as you wanted to hear—no one likes a man who brings bad news!

CREON: If I'd ever thought . . . Who can have dared—

CHORUS *tentatively*: My lord, perhaps one of the Gods—

CREON rounds on him angrily.

CREON: That's enough! D'you want me to lose my temper? You may be old, but that's no reason to talk like a fool! The Gods, indeed! I suppose they honoured him as the saviour of Thebes, this pirate who came to sack their temples and destroy their country! I suppose you think the Gods are fond of criminals!

He controls himself, with an effort.

No, that's not who it was. I've known for some time that there's a group here in the city who oppose me, who meet in secret to shake their heads over what I do, and refuse to accept me as their King. They're the ones responsible—you'll see!—they'll have bribed someone to commit this crime! There's nothing people won't do for money! But this is one thing they won't get away with! You! Guard!

69

GUARD *springing to attention:* Sir!

CREON: Find him: find the criminal and bring him here to me! Otherwise I'll hold you all responsible—as God's my witness I'll have the lot of you tortured until you tell me everything, and find out for yourselves whom to obey in future!

GUARD: Er . . . permission to speak, sir?

CREON: You can tell me nothing I want to hear!

GUARD: Want to hear, sir? Want, or *need*?

CREON: What d'you mean, fellow? Don't split hairs with me!

GUARD: What I mean is, you *need* to hear everything we know—even if you don't *want* to hear us telling you!

CREON: You've got your orders—any questions?

GUARD: Questions, no: I only want to make it clear that I'd nothing to do with it!

CREON: And suppose you had? Suppose you were bribed—

GUARD *in an injured tone:* Sir, how can you think a thing like that?

CREON *grimly:* I'm warning you, my friend: unless you find the criminals, and bring them here to me, that's just what I *shall* think! I'll hold *you* personally responsible!

He goes angrily into the palace. The GUARD *waits until he is out of earshot, and then shouts defiantly after him:*

GUARD: I can only hope the criminals turn up, then! But I'll tell you one thing straight: find them or not, you won't catch *me* here again in a hurry! I didn't think I was going to get out of it alive *this* time, and I'll think twice before I put my neck in a noose a second time!

He hurries out. The CHORUS *now sing an ode in
praise of mankind, and his great intelligence.*

CHORUS:

    I wander tireless over the grey sea
    In storms and winter weather;
    I pass over the waves, braving
    The roar and surge of the waters.

    I toil at the deathless cruel earth,
    The first God: my furrows wrinkle
    Her brown cheeks, as my plough
    Follows the patient horses,
    And the years fall away.

    Speech is mine, and wind-swift thought:
    I have learnt the manners of cities
    And the laws of living together.

    Resourceful and much-contriving,
    I master proud horses: easily
    I snare the wild beasts of the mountains.

    Man am I: the first of wonders.
    I have conquered baffling diseases—
    And yet I am bound by death,
    And the wind mocks my striving.

*

SCENE THREE

The scene is the same. It is some time later. The
GUARD *hurries in eagerly.*

GUARD: We've got her! We've got the one who did it!
Caught her red-handed, burying him! Where's King
Creon?

CHORUS: Here, just coming out of the palace.

CREON *comes in.*

CREON: What is it? What's happened?

GUARD: My lord, it's a great mistake to swear to anything, in case you change your mind afterwards, and end
up a liar! Take me, for instance: the last time I was
here, the time you gave me such a telling-off, I swore
nothing on earth would ever bring me back again! But
now something's happened, something so unexpected that
it's made me forget my oath, and come back after all!

CREON: But what—

GUARD: I've brought you this young lady . . .

He beckons to two SOLDIERS *off-stage, who bring in*
ANTIGONE.

We caught her in the act, burying him!. . . .

Suddenly CREON *realises that he has caught himself
in his own trap. The* GUARD, *unaware of the effect his
story is having, continues eagerly:*

And there was no need to draw lots *this* time, who was to
come! I found her, I did, no one else—and I've brought
her here for you to deal with! All I'm worried about is
clearing myself of having done it!

CREON: You caught her: how?

GUARD: Burying him—it's as simple as that!

CREON *almost in desperation:* Think, man! Do you realise what you're saying?

GUARD *doggedly:* I found her burying the corpse you ordered not to be buried! It seems clear enough to me!

CREON: But how did it happen?

GUARD: It was like this: when we got back, our ears still stinging with your threats, we swept all the dust clear of the corpse, and left him there, lying bare and sodden on the plain. Then we went up on to a little hill (up-wind from him, as he was beginning to stink a bit!) and took up your position there—and you can be sure no one was allowed to take it easy *this* time! You should have heard some of the things—

CREON: Yes, yes; but how did she—

GUARD: I'm coming to that! Nothing happened for quite a while, until the sun was high in the sky, and really blazing down. Then suddenly a great dust-storm blew up, and filled the plain: the leaves were tossing about on the trees, and you had to hold your eyes tight shut to keep the dust out! However, after a bit it blew over—and that's when we saw her, down beside the corpse, scream-ing like a mother bird come home and found her nestlings stolen, and fair cursing whoever it was had swept him clean!

CREON: And then what?

GUARD: She picked up a handful of dust, and started pour-ing out funeral offerings from a bronze urn she had with her. When we saw *that* we nipped down there pretty smartly, I can tell you! She didn't seem frightened, and when we charged her with this, and what she'd done before, she didn't try and deny it. I'm not sure whether to be glad or sorry, really. Glad to be in the clear myself, but sorry to get someone else into trouble! Though—it's only fair to say it—if I had to choose between myself and somebody else—

CREON: All right, that'll do! Antigone . . . Antigone, look at me! Do you admit you did this, or deny it?

ANTIGONE *in a low voice, but firmly:* Yes, I did it. Why should I deny it?

CREON: You! Guard!

GUARD: Sir!

CREON: You can go now—and you're cleared from blame!

GUARD: Sir!

He hurries out in obvious relief, followed by the two SOLDIERS.

CREON: Now, Antigone, answer me this: did you know of my proclamation forbidding this corpse to be buried?

ANTIGONE: Of course I knew. It was plain enough.

CREON: And you dared to disobey?

ANTIGONE: Yes! It wasn't Zeus who made this law, or any other of the Gods—it was you, a mortal! And I thought a mortal's proclamation had no power against the Gods' unwritten laws—laws not made to last a day or a week, but for ever; laws no mortal man could ever make me break!

CREON: But the penalty—

ANTIGONE: Was death! I knew that. But I also knew, without needing a proclamation from you to tell me, that I would have to die one day—and can't you see that the sooner death comes, the happier I'll be? What sort of life do you think I lead? Do you imagine death won't be a

74

blessing when it does come? I tell you I shall bear it easily. What I couldn't bear would be the thought that I'd left my brother, my own mother's son, to rot unburied. Can't you see that? I suppose you think it's foolish—but consider this: which is more foolish, my respect for the Dead, or your law calling it a crime?

CHORUS: She's her father's daughter: the children of Oedipus never know when to give in.

CREON *grimly:* She'll give in! The hardest iron can be melted, the proudest horse bridled—and her spirit can be broken! It's her pride that'll kill her—the pride she showed when she dared to break my laws, the pride she's showing now, boasting about what she's done! I won't tolerate it! I shall punish her as I declared I would!

CHORUS: My lord, your own niece—

CREON: Yes, my niece! If she was my own daughter, she'd still be punished!

He calls to the SERVANTS:

Bring in her sister! I know Ismene had a hand in this: I saw her wandering about inside just now, weeping and wringing her hands like a madwoman! Criminals always give themselves away! I won't let them get away with it—I won't have them caught red-handed and then stand by while they boast about what they've done—as *she's* doing now!

ANTIGONE *quietly:* The penalty was death: will that satisfy you?

CREON: Your death will be enough.

ANTIGONE: Why delay, then? Why not kill me at once? We've nothing more to say to each other. I've buried my brother: is there any greater glory I could wish for? I

75

know everyone in Thebes would agree with me—if they weren't too afraid of *you* to speak out!

CREON *harshly:* That's not true! No one in the city supports you—

ANTIGONE: They all do. They're too frightened to say so, that's all!

CREON: I tell you you're alone! Are you too ashamed to admit it?

ANTIGONE: Ashamed? Ashamed to have buried my own brother?

CREON: And Eteocles, his enemy, who died fighting him—wasn't he your brother too?

ANTIGONE *quietly:* He was.

CREON: And you still don't see how you're dishonouring him by burying his enemy? For Polynices *was* his enemy, brother or no brother!

ANTIGONE: Eteocles would never think so! He would agree with me!

CREON: Not if you treat him the same as a traitor!

ANTIGONE: It won't matter to Eteocles whether his brother was a traitor or not! Can't you see that? All that matters is that it was Polynices he killed—not a stranger or an unknown slave, but his own brother!

CREON: His own brother, perhaps—but one who died attacking Thebes, while *he* defended her!

ANTIGONE: You don't understand! Death makes them equal, and we owe them equal honour!

CREON: Equal honour? A traitor and a hero?

ANTIGONE: The Dead won't distinguish between them!

CREON: Even Death doesn't make an enemy a friend!

ANTIGONE: They were my brothers: how can I love one and hate the other? I love them both!

76

CREON *exasperated:* Love them, then! Join them down in Hell and love them there! I won't be over-ruled by a woman's arguments!

CHORUS: My lord, here comes Ismene from the palace, weeping for her sister.

ISMENE is led in.

CREON: Come here, you viper! Two traitors in the King's own house! Come here! And tell me: did you or did you not have a share in this?

ISMENE: I helped her, and I must share the blame!

She rushes to ANTIGONE.

Oh Antigone, let me say I helped you!

ANTIGONE *coldly:* No: you refused to help me then, and you've no right to try to now. (to CREON) She had nothing to do with it!

ISMENE: I held back then—but now I want to be with you, whatever you have to suffer!

ANTIGONE: It would make no difference to our brothers: *they* know who honoured them! You can't love with words alone—you have to act!

ISMENE: Antigone, Antigone, don't prevent me dying with you, and honouring Polynices too!

ANTIGONE: You refused to honour him earlier, and I won't allow it now! One death—mine—will be enough.

ISMENE: But how can I live without you?

ANTIGONE: Ask Creon: isn't he the one you love?

ISMENE *desperately:* Antigone, I beg you: let me die with you!

ANTIGONE: You chose to live: it was I who chose death!

CREON: The pair of them are mad!

ISMENE *turning to him:* How can I live without her?

77

CREON: You must: she is dead already.

ISMENE: But surely . . . you won't *execute* her?

Desperately she searches in her mind for some new reason.

Creon, she's your own son's bride!

CREON *firmly:* Haemon must find someone else.

ISMENE: But he loves *her*—

CREON: My son will never marry a criminal!

ANTIGONE *bitterly:* Haemon, darling Haemon, how your father hates you!

CREON: It's not Haemon that's your "darling"—it's Polynices! And how well you suit each other!

CHORUS: My lord, will you part your own son from his bride?

CREON *grimly:* Death will part them, not I.

CHORUS: She must die, then?

CREON: Yes, she must! (*to the* SERVANTS) Take them inside! And guard them carefully—even spirits as proud as theirs may try to escape, when they realise just how close death is!

ANTIGONE and ISMENE are led away. CREON remains onstage during the following choral ode.

CHORUS:

Have you ever seen waves, swollen by the storm winds,
Churn up dark sand from the silent depths,
Roll on across the desolate waters, and then crash
And shatter vainly on some stubborn cliff?
Thus fate engulfs the man the Gods have doomed:
His house falls round him; there is no escape.

So falls the house of Thebes: so Laius fell;

So fell his son, unhappy Oedipus—and soon
His children's light will die, quenched by the dust,
The bloodstained dust that covered Polynices;
Quenched by unbending pride; quenched by the Gods.

For where is the man can stand against the Gods?
Sleep, that masters all things, cannot touch them;
Time has not made them grey. They have always been,
And always shall be, rulers of bright Olympus—
What man can challenge them, and hope to win?

*

SCENE FOUR

Scene: the same. CREON *has not moved.*

CHORUS: My lord, here comes Haemon, your youngest
son. I wonder how the news has affected him?
CREON: We'll know soon enough.

HAEMON comes in from the palace.

Haemon, my son, I hope this tragedy hasn't turned you
against me. It wasn't easy for me to condemn your future
bride—but it was unavoidable: I had no choice. Can you
see that?
HAEMON: My lord, I'm your son, and must be ruled by
your advice. If you're against Antigone, that's all there
is to say. I value your good opinion more highly than
any marriage.
CREON: I'm glad to hear you say so. This is what all
fathers pray for, loving and obedient sons—no one ad-

mires a man whose children are rebellious and discontented. I'm glad you haven't let your love for this woman over-rule your better judgement.

HAEMON: Father, you know I'd never willingly disobey you!

CREON: A woman like Antigone would have been cold comfort to you—far better let her find a husband down in Hell! She was found breaking the law, the only traitor in the whole of Thebes: and I must keep my oath, and have her executed, or I'd be betraying the city too! How could I ever punish a stranger, if I let Antigone go free just because she was related to me?

CHORUS: If you want to rule a city justly, you must begin with justice in your own home.

CREON: And you must never break your oath. No one will obey a man who swears to do something, and then changes his mind. And the King *must* be obeyed—obeyed without question, even in the smallest matter. Disobedience destroys cities, breaks up homes, scatters armies, and turns triumph into disaster. No one must disobey the King—and that's why he himself must always keep his word, and do what he swears to do. How could I expect the people of Thebes to follow me, if I promised one thing, and then did another? It would be fatal for me to make an exception of Antigone! Can you understand that?

HAEMON: Yes, father, I can understand it very well—and it would take a wiser man than me to prove you wrong. But I must warn you that not everyone in Thebes agrees with you!

CREON: What do you mean?

HAEMON: I hear things people wouldn't dare say to you.

The King has only to look at a man to silence him: but I'm not the King, and I hear what people are muttering in the shadows—

CREON *a little ironically:* Oh, you do, do you? And what *are* they muttering?

HAEMON: They pity her: they're saying she doesn't deserve to die. They're saying that burying her dead brother wasn't a crime, but that it *would* have been a crime to leave him lying for dogs and birds to nibble at! They're saying she deserves a golden crown for what she's done, not a traitor's death!

CREON: She *must* die! I won't break my oath!

HAEMON: Why not? Even a King can change his mind. It's only fools who think they're never wrong: a wise man is always willing to learn. When a flood sweeps through a forest, the trees that bend, survive: the ones that don't, snap off and are swept away! You can bend, too: you *can* change your mind. A man who knows when to follow good advice is just as sensible as one who never makes mistakes!

CHORUS: My lord, listen to him—

CREON *angrily:* That's enough! Am I to be taught wisdom by a boy his age?

HAEMON: It's not age that matters: it's knowing right from wrong!

CREON: I suppose you'll tell me next that honouring criminals is right!

HAEMON *quietly:* No one in Thebes thinks she's a criminal.

CREON: No one in Thebes! I don't take orders from Thebes!

HAEMON: Now you're the one that's talking like a boy!

CREON: In every state, one man makes the laws—the King!

HAEMON: Do you want to be a King, or a dictator?

CREON: What d'you mean? Are you on this woman's side?

HAEMON: Yes, if *you're* " this woman " ! I'm on no one's side but yours!

CREON: What? When you disagree with everything I say?

HAEMON: Only because you're mistaken!

CREON: Mistaken! To support my own authority! The King doesn't make mistakes!

HAEMON: Even a King must accept the authority of the Gods.

CREON: You dare say that to *me*?

HAEMON: Can't you see what you're doing?

CREON: You're on this woman's side, not mine!

HAEMON: Can't you understand that there aren't *any* sides in this argument? We're all on the same side: you and I, the Gods—yes, and Antigone too!

CREON: Nothing you can say will save her! You'll never marry her alive!

HAEMON: Then she won't be the only one to die!

CREON: Are you threatening me?

HAEMON: I'm only trying to show you how wrong you are!

CREON: Wrong? You'll soon find out who's wrong—and you'll be sorry you ever did! (*to the* SERVANTS) Bring in that viper Antigone! Bring her in and execute her here, where this boy can watch her die!

HAEMON *furiously:* No, never! That's one thing I'll never

do! You won't see me here again! Find others to watch
you play the tyrant—I've seen enough!

He rushes out.

CHORUS: My lord, he's gone out in a fury: and you can
never tell what a young man's fury—
CREON: He can do what he likes! Fury or no fury, he
won't save them!
CHORUS: There's no hope, then—for either of them?
CREON: Antigone must die. But not Ismene: she'd no
hand in it.
CHORUS: And Antigone—how will she die?
CREON: She'll be taken up into the hills, and be sealed
up in a cave, with food enough for a day or two—I won't
have it said that I murdered her! Once she's there, she
can pray to Death, the only God she seems to respect!
She'll soon discover what happens to those who worship
no one else!

He goes into the palace.

CHORUS:
No God, no man, can fight with Love and win—
For he is everywhere: walking the wild sea,
Patrolling the hills and the quiet pastureland;
He sits encamped on a girl's soft cheeks,
To delude the wise, turn fathers from their sons.
One look from him, and Haemon fell:
One glance from his bride's grey eyes defeated him.
Love took the place of a son's duty,
And turned his heart against the Gods—
Love conquered him, and brought him low.

*The SOLDIERS now lead ANTIGONE out from the
palace, and she and the CHORUS begin a mourning song.*

83

CHORUS:

> Weep, weep for Antigone,
> On her last, long journey,
> Meeting a silent bridegroom,
> Marrying unending night.

ANTIGONE:

> I shall make no more journeys now—
> Today I shall watch my last sun die.
> For Death, that makes all men drowsy,
> Is leading me where the dark water
> Laps at the silent shores of night.

CHORUS:

> Weep, weep for Antigone
> Who dared to go too far,
> Driven on by her father's curse
> Till a dark death claimed her.

ANTIGONE:

> No friends are left to weep for me;
> No one is left to sing for me,
> As I started on this, my last journey,
> Going into the darkness, to meet Death
> And join his sombre wedding-feast.

CHORUS:

> Weep, weep for Antigone—

The lament is interrupted by CREON, *who comes in from the palace.*

CREON *coldly:* Weep as much as you like: it won't help you! (*to the* SOLDIERS) Take her away! Take her to her cave! We've done all we could to persuade her she was wrong, without success—and now she can't escape her doom! Take her away!

ANTIGONE:

There is no more to say. A dark bridegroom
Is waiting to welcome me, waiting to greet
The last sad child of Laius' house, last
And most unhappy.
And they are waiting too, waiting with smiles
To greet me in the silent halls of Death:
My father Oedipus, my unhappy mother,
And the brother I loved above life itself.
All of them I buried: at my hands
They received the offerings we owe the Dead.
Was this a crime—was it so criminal
To honour them? Yes! For in Creon's eyes
My brother was a traitor, and his honouring
Has brought me death, and a sombre wedding-day.
If I had lost a husband, or fair children,
And he had stood against their burying,
I should have let them rot: another man
Would soon enough have given me other children.
But this was my own brother, the last hope
Of Oedipus and sad Jocasta—for the Dead
May hope no more for any mortal child.
And for this I must die, unwept, alone,
Unmarried and most miserable.
Which of the Gods have I offended? Which
Of them laid down the laws that I have broken?
None! It was Creon I offended: his
Was the law I dared to break! If he is right,
It is just for the Gods to punish me now,
And I accept their judgement. But if not,
I pray that Creon, too, may taste this cup
Of sorrow, taste it, drain it choking down!

CREON: That's enough! Take her away!

The SOLDIERS *lead her away.*

CHORUS: She'll never give in, and admit she was wrong.

CREON: She won't have another chance! She knew what she was doing, and she must pay the price!

TIRESIAS, *the blind prophet, is led in by his* BOY.

TIRESIAS: Gentlemen, we have travelled here together, the boy and I, with one pair of eyes to guide us both.

CREON: Sir, you are welcome. Have you come with news for us, or on some other errand? What is it that's brought you here?

TIRESIAS: I've come to bring you news, news and advice.

CREON: I've always been guided by your advice, my lord.

TIRESIAS: Then listen to me now: for you're standing on a razor's edge!

CREON: A razor's edge? What do you mean?

TIRESIAS: Listen, and I'll tell you what happened. I was sitting in my ancient place of prophecy, when suddenly I heard a strange, wild sound: birds, screaming madly overhead, flapping their wings wildly, and tearing at each other with their talons, till the whole sky was filled with their cries. I was sure it was the sign of some approaching tragedy, and I went to sacrifice and ask the Gods' advice. The altar was heaped ready with kindling: but when I tried to light it, it refused to burn. Instead, a hideous liquid mess began trickling down, sputtering and hissing in the ashes, till there was nothing left of the sacrifice but scattered bones.

CREON: But what did it signify, this dreadful omen?

TIRESIAS: Simply this: King Creon has brought a curse on Thebes!

86

CREON *angrily:* A curse? What curse?

TIRESIAS: Birds and dogs have defiled our altars, defiled them with flesh torn from Polynices! And so long as he lies unburied, the Gods will refuse to accept our offerings; so long as the birds are gorged with his flesh, there are no good omens they can give us!

CREON: I don't understand: how can a traitor's death disgust the Gods?

TIRESIAS: Take my word for it, it does! Think carefully, my lord: everyone makes mistakes, but a wise man makes up for them by trying to put them right—only fools stand firm when they know they're wrong!

CREON: And *I'm* the one that's wrong! Is that what you mean?

TIRESIAS: You've let your hatred of Polynices go too far! He's dead now—he can't do you any further harm. You're trying to kill him twice over!

CREON: So your advice—

TIRESIAS:—is only for your good, and the good of Thebes!

CREON is clearly struggling to keep his temper.

CREON: My lord Tiresias, in every state the easiest target when things go wrong, is the ruler himself. Even *you're* using me as a scapegoat now, making up prophecies to try to frighten me! Who bribed you to say this? Who paid you to betray me?

TIRESIAS: Bribed me? Paid me? What talk is this?

CREON: Not all the wealth of Sardis, not all the gold of India, will buy him burial! You say he disgusts the Gods, lying there rotting on the plain—well, I tell you: not even if the eagles carried him up to rot on the door-

87

step of Zeus himself, would I give in to you! No mortal, dead or alive, can disgust the Gods—they pay no heed to traitors!

TIRESIAS: You're talking like a madman!

CREON: Be careful! Even wise men and prophets can be punished when they twist good into evil, and take bribes to hide the truth!

TIRESIAS *with a sigh*: Ah, can any man say he's wise, and know for certain that he's right?

CREON: Fine words! But what exactly do they mean?

TIRESIAS: Wisdom is the greatest blessing a man can have.

CREON: Yes—and foolishness is the greatest curse!

TIRESIAS: A curse you yourself are suffering from!

CREON: I won't argue with you—it's wrong to quarrel with a prophet.

TIRESIAS: And yet you say my prophecies are lies!

CREON: All I'm saying is that every priest loves money!

TIRESIAS: And I'm saying there's no King will ever admit he's wrong!

CREON: Do you realise it's a King you're talking to?

TIRESIAS: A King, yes—but one who relies on me to help him rule!

CREON *scornfully*: Relies on *you*—a man who prophesies for money?

TIRESIAS: Be careful! I haven't told you everything.

CREON: Tell me whatever you like—but don't expect any reward for it!

TIRESIAS: You still think I was bribed to come?

CREON: Yes! And you can tell your employer you've failed! You'll never change my mind!

TIRESIAS *grimly*: Very well. Listen to me, now. I solemnly

swear to you, that before the sun has come and gone, your son—your own son—will be sacrificed to pay your debts to the Dead: once, for the life you've sent to a living grave, and once for the corpse you refused to honour. There's no avoiding it: not long from now your palace and your city will be filled with weeping—and the pollution will spread, carried by the animals and carrion birds that have fed on Polynices, until all the states round Thebes rise up and come to destroy her. You can't escape. What you've done must earn its just reward.

He turns to find his BOY.

Boy! Take me home! Some younger man can stay and face his fury; someone else can wait for him to check his tongue, and learn a little wisdom!

He goes out with his BOY, *leaving* CREON *completely crushed.*

CHORUS: My lord, this was a terrible prophecy!
CREON: Terrible . . .
CHORUS: In all the years since I was a boy, I've never known him wrong!
CREON: I know . . . I know . . . it's horrible . . . to yield . . . or stand and watch your fate creeping up on you . . . coming to overwhelm you . . .
CHORUS: You must listen to our advice, now.
CREON: Advice . . . yes . . .
CHORUS: You must free Antigone, my lord: free her, and give her brother burial!
CREON *helplessly:* Free her? You think so? You advise me to . . . to give way?
CHORUS: My lord, I do—and quickly, before the Gods have time to act!

CREON: Very well . . . if there's no other way . . . I must give in . . .

CHORUS: Go now! Go yourself and do it! Don't leave it to someone else!

CREON: Yes . . . yes . . . you're right . . .

With an effort he pulls himself together, and calls to the SERVANTS.

All of you, quickly: bring spades and axes with you! To the hills—and hurry! (*to the* CHORUS) I shut her in; I must free her . . . there's no other way . . . a man must obey the Gods . . .

He stumbles out. The CHORUS, *in the belief that all is now well, sing a hymn in praise of Bacchus, the patron God of Thebes.*

CHORUS:

Lord of the dancing stars, fair son of Zeus,
The glory of our sunburnt Theban plain,
Lord Bacchus, from the rustling vines, the hills
And silent forests, come and dance for us!

For Thebes, loveliest of cities, lies sick:
The Gods have sent a plague to gnaw at her.
The mountains are shrouding their heads in grief,
And Euripus' sacred stream is weeping for her.

Take pity on us, son of Zeus: come down
And fill our peaceful meadowland with dancing.
Come down to us: let us dance, till we waken
The startled dawn with revelry—Bacchus, come!

*

SCENE FIVE

Scene: the same. As the CHORUS *finish their song, a* MESSENGER *rushes breathlessly in.*

MESSENGER: Citizens of Thebes, I bring you news of King Creon!

CHORUS: What news? Is the King . . . dead?

MESSENGER: Not dead, no—but suffering a living death! He's still the King, still a wealthy man—but what use are wealth and power to him now? He'll never find happiness again!

CHORUS: Why? What happened? Tell us, quickly!

MESSENGER: Haemon is dead—and by his own hand!

CHORUS *aghast:* His own hand!

MESSENGER: And as he killed himself, he screamed at Creon that *he* was responsible!

CHORUS: Just as Tiresias foretold . . .

MESSENGER: Our whole life's collapsing in ruins; we must try and save ourselves . . .

EURYDICE, *the Queen, comes out of the palace.*

EURYDICE *anxiously:* Gentlemen, I was on my way to pray in Athene's temple, when word reached me of some terrible tragedy, and I hurried out for clearer news. Tell me what's happened!

MESSENGER: My lady, I was there, and I saw it all . . .

EURYDICE: Tell me everything!

MESSENGER: But, madam . . .

EURYDICE: Don't try to spare my feelings!

MESSENGER: Very well, my lady: the truth is always best. This is what happened. I went with your husband, the King, out across the plain to where Polynices was lying—or as much of him as the dogs had left. We washed the remains in holy water, and burnt them with the usual funeral prayers and offerings. Then, when we'd buried his ashes under a mound of earth, we left him, and went to find his sister in her rocky death-chamber. We were still some way off, when we heard the sound of terrible, hopeless weeping from inside the cave. Some-one ran and told the King, and, as he came nearer and heard the bitter sobbing, he shouted despairingly: "My son's voice! Pray God we're not too late! Some of you —hurry!—go and pull the rocks away from the cave-mouth, and see whether it really is Haemon, or whether the Gods are mocking me!"

EURYDICE: And you obeyed?

MESSENGER: Yes. We went and pulled the stones away. And then we saw her—Antigone—hanging, dead, in a corner of the cave, in a noose made from strips of her own clothing!

EURYDICE: And Haemon? Where was he?

MESSENGER: Standing beside her, with his arms round her poor strangled corpse, weeping and lamenting for his dead bride, his marriage hopes, ruined by his father's cruelty. When the King saw him, he rushed towards him, crying: "Haemon, Haemon! My son, what have you done? Why did you come here? I beg you, come away from here! Come home with me!" The boy just looked at him, his eyes flashing with hatred; then suddenly he spat, full in his father's face—and before we could stop him he pulled out his sword and struck hard at Creon. The King jumped out of the way . . .

He pauses, and then continues slowly:

. . . and Haemon turned the sword against himself, thrusting it home into his own ribs. Then, with blood gushing and bubbling out of his mouth, he kissed Antigone for the last time, so that her pale cheeks were stained crimson with his blood. And there they lie, together, bride and groom, married at last in death: a proof for us all of the terrible results of human folly!

He turns to the Queen; but she has quietly gone into the palace, unnoticed by everybody.

CHORUS: What can it mean? The Queen's hurried out, without a word!

MESSENGER: I don't know. I hope it means nothing more than this: that she's too proud to show her grief in public, and has gone inside to weep and mourn for Haemon privately.

But suddenly, he, too, realises the other awful possibility, and speaks with horror in his voice.

She wouldn't do *anything else*? . . .

CHORUS: She might! I don't like her silence—it's unnatural!

MESSENGER: Yes, it *is* ominous! I'll go in and make sure nothing's happened!

As he goes into the palace, a sad procession makes its way in from the plain, led by CREON, *and servants bearing the body of* HAEMON.

CREON:
We have come back, the two of us,
Murderer and victim, the father
And the young son he killed,
Crushed by the pitiless hand of God.

CHORUS: You have learned wisdom, but learned it too late.

CREON:

I have learned wisdom, and the knowledge crushes me.
The Gods have struck me down, shattered my life
And turned my happiness to hopeless misery.

The MESSENGER *comes running out of the palace.*

MESSENGER: My lord, this tragedy is not the last:
There is still more, inside, for you to bear!

CREON: Still more? Could there be more, worse than this?

MESSENGER: My lord, the Queen, his mother, has taken her own life.

CREON:

O Death,
Will nothing satisfy you yet?
I died when Haemon died—and now
I must die again with Eurydice!
How did it happen? Where is she?

The palace doors are thrown open, to reveal the body of EURYDICE.

CHORUS: Here, my lord. They have opened the palace doors.

CREON *suddenly shouts, in a terrible cry of bitterness:*

CREON:

If there is more to bear, I will not bear it!
This is enough! My son lies dead in my arms,
And inside, his mother, too, is dead! I've seen enough!

MESSENGER:

Two sons she mourned, while the sword drank her blood:

Her eldest, dead in the Theban wars, and now
Her youngest, Haemon, slaughtered too. She fell,
And as darkness snatched at her, she cursed you:
  Cursed the King, her husband, and her son's murderer!

CREON:

  O Zeus,
  I am tainted with disaster—
  Will you not kill me, too?
  I long for Death, the dark lord,
  To come, and end my suffering!

MESSENGER:

  You caused their deaths: as the Queen's last breath
  Rattled in her throat, she laid the blame on you!

CREON:

  How did she die?

MESSENGER: She heard of Haemon's death,
  How he buried his sword deep in his own body,
  And she chose to walk the same road herself.

CREON *in sudden fury:*

  Why?
  Why have the Gods cursed me?
  I killed them! I was the one
  Who ended their sweet lives! Why?
  Why is all I touch accursed?

  Suddenly he begins laughing and shouting like a mad-man.

  Slaves! Take me away from here! I have died, too,
  And must lie down in darkness! Take me away!

CHORUS *sadly:* This is the only way left, the quickest
  and the best.

95

CREON:

O Death,
Death, sweet lord, come for me now !
Come now, and lead me home.
I have infected all I touched,
And fate has crushed me utterly !
Take me away !

He is led away. On the bare stage, the CHORUS *are left alone.*

CHORUS:

The greatest gifts a man can have
Are Wisdom and the fear of Heaven.
Man's pride will always be punished,
And all his boastfulness brought low.

*

3

THE ACHARNIANS

NOTE

Many authorities believe that *The Acharnians* is Aristophanes' finest play. Whether this be true or not, it is without doubt one of the best-constructed of them all, and combines serious thought with extravagant burlseque to an extent unparalleled in his other works. The tragic parodies[1] in this play are particularly excellent: Aristophanes' favourite butt, Euripides, is taken as the model for an unusually large number of pseudo-tragic lines, especially in the brilliant closing contest between Dikaiopolis and the braggart general Lamachos (p. 142)—and the scene where Euripides himself appears, in a hip-bath, in the throes of dramatic composition (p. 119), is generally considered to be one of the finest in all Greek comedy.

In some ways the exuberance of *The Acharnians* is a result of the desperate situation in which it was written. The two great speeches of Dikaiopolis (his opening speech, p. 102, and the one delivered from the gallows, p. 124) exactly sum up the plight of Athens in 425, when *The Acharnians* won first prize in the dramatic contest. Everywhere in the city there was poverty and despair, and affairs were 'controlled' by upstart leaders and crooked generals, whose only concern was to fight as little as possible, and make as much money as they could by extortion and intimidation. Out of these circumstances the play was born. The assembly scene at the beginning, in which no views are allowed but those of the official party, is probably very close to what actually went on at the time; and the Megarian

[1] In this play, as in *Peace*, passages which parody Euripides' style are given in inverted commas.

scene, too (p. 131) shows a real understanding of the sufferings of innocent people under the conditions of war. Aristophanes was no pacifist—he supported 'just wars'—but he fought all his life against people who used war conditions for their own advancement.

Both in this play, and in the Hermes scene in *Peace*, Aristophanes makes use of the flat roof of the stage-building. In this play it is used to represent the upstairs floor of a house, and in *Peace* it represents the door of Heaven. Trygaios, in *Peace*, gets up to it by means of the crane which was a common feature of the Greek theatre; in *The Acharnians* a section of scenery is rotated out of the way, to show Euripides in his bath, dictating tragedies to his slave.

It is easy to think of Aristophanes as nothing more than a writer of farce; but this play, more than any of the others he wrote, shows that this is not the true picture. He used farce as a cloak for seriousness : like all true satirists, he made his point through ridicule. In Dikaiopolis' gallows speech, despite the comic surroundings, he lays bare his true intentions, which are to shock the Athenians out of their apathy and despair, and make them once again the leaders of Greece. The difficulty of this task can be imagined from the depths of despair in which they are shown in the Assembly at the beginning of the play, where frauds and cheats are allowed to go unchallenged, and the officials can pass whatever laws they like, without encountering any opposition.

The play begins with Dikaiopolis waiting for the start of this Assembly. . . .

THE ACHARNIANS

Characters:

Speaking parts:
DIKAIOPOLIS, *an Athenian citizen*
EURIPIDES, *a tragic poet*
Euripides' SLAVE
LAMACHOS, *a braggart general*
Lamachos' SLAVE
MEGARIAN
His two DAUGHTERS
BOEOTIAN, *a spiv*
NIKARCHOS, *an informer*
AMPHITHEOS, *a God*
HERALD
AMBASSADOR
THEOROS, *a diplomat*
PSEUDARTABAS, *a Persian*

CHORUS of *Acharnians, led by* DIKASTES,
   POLYPRAGMON *and* LAKRATEIDES

Non-speaking parts:

XANTHIAS, *Dikaiopolis' slave*
ISMENIAS, *the Boeotian's slave.*
The ODOMANTIAN ARMY
Policemen, Townspeople, Officials, Musicians, etc.

THE ACHARNIANS

SCENE ONE

The backcloth represents a street in Athens, and shows the doors of three houses, those of DIKAIOPOLIS, LAMACHOS and EURIPIDES. EURIPIDES' house is the last in the street, and beyond it the city walls can be seen in the distance: their gates are closed, and protected behind piles of sandbags, and the walls themselves are patrolled by sentries. Occasionally trumpet calls and galloping hooves can be heard; but the street, and the square beyond it (the assembly-place) are deserted and silent. DIKAIOPOLIS is sitting with his back to the wall of EURIPIDES' house, facing the deserted assembly-place, and idly tossing stones from one hand to the other. Suddenly he gets up angrily.

DIKAIOPOLIS: No, it's no good! I won't stand it a minute longer! They called an assembly here for ten o'clock this morning—ten o'clock *sharp*—and I thought I'd better get here early to be sure of a seat. "Something of importance for Athens will be discussed", they said—so I got here at ten to nine! And I've been sitting here ever since. It's well after half-past eleven now, and still no sign of our noble counsellors: lingering over their coffee and gossip in the market-place, I'll be bound! You'd think, after seven years of war, that people would come running as soon as there was any prospect of making peace: but no, not a bit of it! I've been here—alone— for nearly three hours now, with nothing else to do but stretch and scratch, scribble rude words in the dust, and look out over the battlements at the countryside: and there hasn't been a soul around in all that time! Ah, the countryside! That's the place to be! No rationing there; no snapping up of all the titbits for greedy generals and corrupt politicians! You grew all you ever wanted on your own home farm—no need to queue for hours, or argue about the price of a cabbage, in the country! I tell you, it's enough to make a man sick, this city life! (*confidentially*) And don't imagine I'm going to let them get away with it this time! As soon as the assembly starts, I'm going to interrupt and shout at the speakers if they mention anything but peace!

People start arriving in twos and threes: first the ordinary TOWNSFOLK, *then the* OFFICIALS *in their magnificent robes of office.*

Ah! Here they come at last! At least, here come the ordinary folk: no sign of the officials yet . . . Oh no, here they are—fighting and jostling to get the best seats on the front row! Twelve o'clock! It's enough to make you sick!

The HERALD *begins organising the crowd.*

HERALD: Move further in, there! (*to* DIKAIOPOLIS) You! Move inside the sacred area—quickly!

Before DIKAIOPOLIS *can retort,* AMPHITHEOS *hurries in—unobserved by the* HERALD, *who has moved on to "organise" someone else.* AMPHITHEOS *is fantastically dressed, and is very much out of breath.*

AMPHITHEOS: H'mmmm-haaa-pffff-arghhh! Has anyone . . . h'mm-pff-argh! . . . anyone . . . pfffff! . . . spoken yet?

HERALD *without looking round:* Why? Who wants to speak?

AMPHITHEOS: *Pfffff-haaargh!* . . . I do! . . . *Arghhh-pfffff!*

HERALD *over his shoulder:* You do, do you? And who *are* you?

AMPHITHEOS *proudly:* Am . . . *pfffff!* . . . phitheos!

Now the HERALD *looks round, and nearly jumps out of his skin.*

HERALD: My God! Is it human?

AMPHITHEOS *offended: Human?* Of course not! I'm a God, and don't you forget it!

HERALD *gaping:* A God?

AMPHITHEOS:

Yes, a God! *(very quickly):*
Here I give you my Godly family-TREE:
Triptolemos begat Amphitheos
Who then begat great Keleos
Whose son was next Lykinos who
In turn himself had soon begotten . . .

Pause: and this is the climax—

ME! !

He bows low.

I'm a God, then: and the other Gods have chosen me to come down here and make peace between you and Sparta. And I may say—

HERALD *angrily:* You've said enough! Sergeant! Throw him out!

Two burly POLICEMEN *struggle with* AMPHITHEOS.

104

AMPHITHEOS: Help! Keleos! Triptolemos!

But his ancestors fail to help him, and he is thrown out.

DIKAIOPOLIS: Gentlemen, what sort of assembly is this, when you throw out the one person in it who was interested in making peace? Is that fair, I ask you?

HERALD *still ruffled:* Sit down! Be quiet!

Fanfare.

Stand forth the ambassadors from the Great King!

DIKAIOPOLIS: Great King? What Great King? Ugh, they make me sick, these ambassadors, with their peacock feathers and their almighty boasting!

HERALD: Be quiet! Sit down!

Another fanfare.

The ambassadors from Persia!

Two gorgeously-dressed black SLAVES swagger in, followed by a giant figure with a single eye painted in the middle of his forehead—PSEUDARTABAS—who is himself followed by another black SLAVE bearing his scimitar. Lastly, the AMBASSADOR.

DIKAIOPOLIS *aside:* Good lord, whatever next! Look at the way they walk!

The party bows to the assembly.

AMBASSADOR *pompously:* Gentlemen, you sent us forth to fare to Persia and see the Great King, when Euthymenes was President of the Council. Our diurnal stipend was two drachmas.

DIKAIOPOLIS *aside:* Poor old drachmas!

AMBASSADOR: We wore ourselves out wandering by the Kayustrian river, sleeping in tents, and riding—in great hardship—upon silk sedans . . .

DIKAIOPOLIS *aside:* You should have been at home in comfort with me, doing guard-duty on the battlements!

AMBASSADOR: Our hosts compelled us to choke down sweet white wine, served in beakers of glass and gold . . .

DIKAIOPOLIS *aside:* O Athens, can't you hear your ambassadors mocking you?

AMBASSADOR: After three years of this intolerable hardship, we came to the Great King's palace, and were welcomed with a mighty feast—oxen roasted whole in the frying-pan . .

DIKAIOPOLIS *aside:* Roasted in the *frying-pan?* What rubbish!

AMBASSADOR: The Great King showed us many wonderful things, and entertained us royally for twelve months; then he sent us back to you, bringing with us Pseudartabas, the Eye of the Great King.

DIKAIOPOLIS *aside:* Eye of the Great King, my foot! It's a pack of lies from beginning to end!

AMBASSADOR: Gentlemen, the Eye of the Great King—in person!

PSEUDARTABAS *salaams deeply to the assembly.*

DIKAIOPOLIS *aside:*   Phew!

"Good lord, sir, what an eye thou blink'st amain!"—to put it like someone out of Euripides! What a peeper!

AMBASSADOR: Come, now, Pseudartabas: tell the assembly what the Great King ordered you to say.

PSEUDARTABAS *with an elaborate gesture:* Holiness-moses-oh-my-goodness-yes!

He steps back, looking very pleased with himself.

AMBASSADOR: Did you follow what he said?

DIKAIOPOLIS: Heavens, no! Not me, at any rate!

AMBASSADOR: He said that the Great King is sending gold to you. Come on, Pseudartabas, say "gold" again, louder!

PSEUDARTABAS *as before:* No-goldly-stupid-fool-Atheni-ass!

Steps back as before.

DIKAIOPOLIS: Well, I certainly got *that* bit!

AMBASSADOR *nastily:* Oh you did, did you? Well then, perhaps you'll tell us what he said.

DIKAIOPOLIS: He said—quite clearly, too—that the Athenians are stupid asses if they expect to get any gold out of the Persians!

AMBASSADOR *hastily:* No, no! He spoke of . . . er . . . *pools* and *flasks* of gold!

DIKAIOPOLIS: Pools and flasks? D'you really expect us to believe that? Clear off, and let me ask the questions! Now, Pseudartabas, give me a straight answer, yes or no, if you don't want all three eyes blacked! Is the Great King going to send us gold?

PSEUDARTABAS *shakes his head violently.*

Well, then, are the ambassadors liars?

PSEUDARTABAS *nods vigorously.*

Well, that seems clear enough to me! What d'you say to *that*, ambassador?

AMBASSADOR *hastily:* No, no, you don't understand . . . er . . . they do things the opposite way round in Persia

107

. . . they nod for "no", and shake their heads for "yes"! . . . er . . . if you follow me!

DIKAIOPOLIS: You don't expect me to believe *that*, do you? You're nothing but a fraud—I don't believe you ever went to Persia in the first place!

HERALD: Sit down! Be QUIET!

He nods to the Trumpeter, who blows another fanfare.

The Council of the City of Athens invites the Eye of the Great King to lunch in the Town Hall!

The AMBASSADOR, PSEUDARTABAS and the SLAVES bow to the assembly, and then walk pompously out.

DIKAIOPOLIS *aside:* Huh! To lunch! It's enough to make a man hang himself! Here am I wasting my time up here, while the Town Hall doors are flung wide open to welcome frauds and liars!

Pause. Suddenly he snaps his fingers with excitement.

But I've just had an idea! . . . Yes, yes, what a beauty! I'll do it!

He hisses into the wings.

Psst! Pssssst! Amphitheos!

AMPHITHEOS creeps in, looking round nervously to make sure the policemen are nowhere near.

AMPHITHEOS *from the side:* Ssssst! Over here!

DIKAIOPOLIS gives him some money.

DIKAIOPOLIS: My friend, I'd like you to take these eight drachmas, and go off to Sparta and buy me a private peace treaty there: one just big enough for me, the wife and the kids, and no one else!

AMPHITHEOS: One private treaty? With pleasure!

He hurries out. Fanfare.

HERALD: Stand forth Theoros, newly returned from the court of King Sitalkes!

THEOROS swaggers in, dressed in full-scale diplomatic uniform. He bows deeply.

DIKAIOPOLIS *aside*: H'mm! Another fraud!

THEOROS *clearing his throat pompously*: H'rrrm! H'rrrm! Hmmmmph! Gentlemen, we would not have lingered so long in Thrace . . .

DIKAIOPOLIS *aside*: If you hadn't been well rewarded!

THEOROS: . . . if the whole of that country had not been covered in snow, and all the rivers frozen over!

DIKAIOPOLIS *aside*: He makes it sound like " Oedipus on Ice! "

THEOROS: My lords, I spent this time drinking with King Sitalkes, and I was so successful at winning his friendship that he swore a great oath to come and help us, with an army so big you'd think a plague of locusts was on the horizon!

DIKAIOPOLIS *aside*: Damn it, I don't believe a word of it, apart from the locusts!

THEOROS: And now he's sent you the most warlike tribe in Thrace . . .

DIKAIOPOLIS *sarcastically, aside*: Oh, naturally!

HERALD: Stand forth the Thracians brought by Theoros!

To the sound of a vilely out-of-tune march, a veritable Falstaff's army staggers in: four ragged soldiers, of all shapes and sizes, with notched swords and tattered clothes. They look too exhausted for anything, but manage to stand—more or less—to attention when their leader barks an order.

DIKAIOPOLIS: What on earth d'you call *these?*

THEOROS *proudly:* This is the great Odomantian Army.

DIKAIOPOLIS: The Odomantian army? H'mmm. They certainly are *odd!*

THEOROS: All you have to do is pay them two drachmas a day, and they'll overrun the whole of Boeotia!

DIKAIOPOLIS: Two drachmas a day? *This* lot? I wouldn't give them a bent farthing to overrun my back garden!

This is too much for the Army: they gather themselves together, make a sortie, and steal DIKAIOPOLIS' *lunchbox.*

Oh, good lord, I'm done for! They've pinched my lunch! (*to the army*) Put it down! Down, I say! DOWN!

THEOROS: You fool! Keep back! They're savage, once they've tasted garlic! Keep your distance!

DIKAIOPOLIS *turns to the assembly.*

DIKAIOPOLIS: Gentlemen, will you sit there and let me be robbed in my own city—and by a pack of foreigners, at that? Stop the assembly! This has gone far enough!

Uproar. Shouts of "traitor", "throw him out", etc. Suddenly DIKAIOPOLIS *has a brainwave. He rushes to his front door and fetches a garden hose, and begins spraying the assembly with it.*

HERALD: Help! It's starting to rain! Dismiss the assembly! We'll all be soaked!

The assembly breaks up in confusion as people rush for shelter—led, of course, by the OFFICIALS. The HERALD tries to make himself heard above the uproar.

Stand down the Thracians! Let them return the day after tomorrow! The officials declare the assembly over!

Gradually the stage clears, and DIKAIOPOLIS is left alone with his hose, but without his lunch-box.

DIKAIOPOLIS: Oh dear, I'm ruined! They've stolen all my lunch! Now what am I going to do?

AMPHITHEOS hurries in, all the time glancing fearfully over his shoulder. He is carrying three bottles: small, medium-sized and large. He is still out of breath, and seems very upset.

AMPHITHEOS: Oh dear, oh dear! They'll tear me to bits! Why did I ever come to earth at all?
DIKAIOPOLIS: Amphitheos! You're back! Have you been to Sparta?
AMPHITHEOS: Ssssh! Can't stop! They're after me!
DIKAIOPOLIS: Who're after you? What's the matter?
AMPHITHEOS *struggling to get away:* No, no! Let me go! They'll murder me!
DIKAIOPOLIS: Who'll murder you? What are you talking about?
AMPHITHEOS: The Acharnians! I was walking along, minding my own business, and bringing you your treaties, when suddenly some old gentleman from Acharni started coming after me: stout, gnarled old oaken gentlemen, the

111

sort who beat the Persians at Marathon! They kept shouting: "Hey, you! You sir, egad! What have you got there? Is that a treaty we can smell? Have you been fraternising with the enemy? What, what?" And then they started filling their cloaks with stones, so I ran away as fast—

DIKAIOPOLIS: Did you get much of a start?

AMPHITHEOS: A bit. Why?

DIKAIOPOLIS: Good: that means I've got time to inspect the treaties! Where are they?

AMPHITHEOS: Here . . . but . . . but—

DIKAIOPOLIS: Come on! Five minutes won't kill you!

He hands DIKAIOPOLIS *the smallest bottle.*

Try that: it's a five-year truce.

DIKAIOPOLIS *takes off the cork and sniffs.*

DIKAIOPOLIS: Ugh! No, that's no good! Not big enough—it smells of secret ship-building, and the hiding away of arms! It's no use to me!

AMPHITHEOS: Well, what about this one? This is a ten-year plan.

Same business with the medium bottle.

DIKAIOPOLIS: No, no, that's no good either! It smells of ambassadors going round trying to stir up the allies, and everyone holding themselves ready to start fighting again as soon as it's finished!

AMPHITHEOS *hands him the largest bottle.*

AMPHITHEOS: Well, try this: it's a thirty-year vintage peace by sea and land.

112

DIKAIOPOLIS: Dionysus, what a lovely smell! Ambrosia and nectar . . . flourishing crops . . . peace and plenty everywhere! Yes, I'll take this one! We'll hold a sacrifice, and then drink it down, and never have anything to worry about again! Thank you, thank you, Amphitheos—I've no more problems now, thanks to you!

He goes joyfully into his house. AMPHITHEOS *is about to follow him, when the sound of an approaching hue-and-cry is heard.*

AMPHITHEOS: Oo-er! I wish I'd no more problems! Here come the Acharnians! I'm off!

He hurries out.

*

SCENE TWO

The scene is the same. As soon as AMPHITHEOS *is out of sight, the* CHORUS *of Acharnians come noisily in, carrying sticks and stones. They are old men, with a military look about them, and they are led by* DIKAS-TES, POLYPRAGMON *and* LAKRATEIDES.

CHORUS:
This way! Quickly! Where's he gone?
We'll soon change his tune for him!
Make him grovel down with fear,
And weep for us to spare his life!
This way! Quickly! Where's—

DIKASTES: Phew! Just a moment—stop here a minute! I'm quite worn out!

LAKRATEIDES: It's no use going any further: we've lost him! He's sneaked off somewhere—we'll never find him now!

POLYPRAGMON *to the audience:* Ladies and gentlemen, did any of you see a shifty-looking character running past with his arms full of treaty-bottles?

DIKASTES: He's for it when we catch him! Filthy traitor!

Suddenly they freeze, as the sound of DIKAIOPOLIS' *voice is heard from inside his house.*

DIKAIOPOLIS *off:* The wine's being poured! Keep silence!

LAKRATEIDES: That's him! That's the man!

POLYPRAGMON: How dare he sacrifice to Peace, before our very noses?

DIKASTES: He's in for it now!

The door of DIKAIOPOLIS' *house opens, and he comes out, leading a procession. He is carrying an altar; his* DAUGHTER *follows him with a basket of barley, and* XANTHIAS, *his slave, brings up the rear with a wine-skin and the treaty-bottle. The* CHORUS *cower down in their dancing-place, so as not to be seen, and watch what follows.*

DIKAIOPOLIS *very excitedly:* That's right! Bring the basket over here, my darling! Xanthias, where's the wine-skin? Good! Is everything ready? Let's begin the sacrifice!

He pours a libation from the wine-skin, saying the usual chant:

The wine's being poured! Keep silence:
And pray that the omens be good!

Splendid! Now, let us pray to Peace.

But any further sacrificing is prevented by the
C H O R U S, *who rush to attack him.*

C H O R U S : Traitor! Spy! Coward! Stone him,
Beat him, drive him out of town!
Traitor! Spartan-lover! Kill him now!

D I K A I O P O L I S : Heracles, what's going on? **Careful!**
You'll spill the wine!

L A K R A T E I D E S *wildly:* Beat him up! Stone him, the
traitor! Kill, kill, kill, kill, kill!

D I K A I O P O L I S : Hey, steady, grandad! What's the
matter? What have I done?

D I K A S T E S : You dare ask us *that*, you traitor? You go
off and make a private treaty with the Spartans, and
then expect us not to come after you? What d'you think
we're made of?

D I K A I O P O L I S : Hot air, by the sound of it! Calm down,
can't you?

P O L Y P R A G M O N : Calm down, he says! Stone him!
Stone him now!

L A K R A T E I D E S : Kill, kill, kill, kill, k—

D I K A I O P O L I S : Just a moment, just a moment! Don't
you want to know *why* I made the treaty? Doesn't that
interest you at all?

D I K A S T E S : The reasons don't matter! All that matters is that you're a traitor, and you've earned a traitor's
death!

P O L Y P R A G M O N : You don't expect us to listen to a man
who makes treaties with the enemy, do you?

115

LAKRATEIDES: Kill, kill, kill, ki—

He is suddenly interrupted: for XANTHIAS, *in response to a sign from* DIKAIOPOLIS, *has crept up behind him, and now jumps on him and bustles him into the house.*

Help! He-e-elp!

DIKASTES: He's captured Lakrateides! Quick! After him!

DIKAIOPOLIS: Steady, steady: not so fast! One false move and I'll tell my slave to let him have it! "Kill!"— is that what he keeps shouting?

POLYPRAGMON: But you wouldn't—

DIKAIOPOLIS: Just you try me!

The CHORUS *confer hastily among themselves. Then* DIKASTES *and* POLYPRAGMON *slowly approach* DIKAIOPOLIS.

That's far enough! Not a step further! What d'you want now?

DIKASTES *with what he hopes is a winning smile:* Er . . . won't you spare his life, sir? We've been friends for nearly sixty years now . . . I couldn't bear . . . er . . . we admit we were perhaps a little hasty just now . . .

POLYPRAGMON: Please don't touch him, sir . . . I beg you . . .

DIKAIOPOLIS: That's more like it! I thought that'd soon stop your nonsense! Now will you listen to me?

DIKASTES: But what is it you want to tell us?

DIKAIOPOLIS: I want to explain just *why* I made peace with the Spartans—and perhaps when you've heard my reasons, you'll agree that it wasn't such treachery after all! Now, will you listen or won't you?

POLYPRAGMON: It's no use: you'll never convince us!

DIKAIOPOLIS: Look: I'm prepared to do it properly, like a character in a tragedy—with torn clothes and ashes on my head. I'll even put my neck in a noose for you, so that if I don't convince you, you can kill me at once! Is that fair?

DIKASTES: It sounds fair enough—but I warn you you're as good as committing suicide! You'll never convince us!

DIKAIOPOLIS: Maybe not: but I'm still going to try. Now go back to your places, while I get everything ready.

The CHORUS *go grumbling back to the dancing-place, and sit down. Meanwhile, as* XANTHIAS *comes back out of the house, carrying a gallows,* DIKAIOPOLIS *addresses the audience.*

Well, now I've done it! Whatever made me say that? I've no choice but to go through with it, now! And in a tragic costume, too! Wherever can I get hold of one of those? It'll have to be a good one—they're going to take a lot of convincing! (*pondering*) Now where . . .

Suddenly he has a brainwave.

I know: Euripides! He'll lend me everything I need! . . . But it's no good asking him in an ordinary way: he only seems to understand proper tragic language! Now, what's the best way to approach him? . . .

He braces himself for action, then strikes several different tragic poses by way of experiment. Eventually he finds one he likes, and declaims:

" The hour has come for action: now I know it!
I must go seek Euripides, the tragic poet! "

He goes up to Euripides' house.

" I'll knock. Halloo ! Who is within? "

He knocks. The door is opened—grandly—by Euripides'
SLAVE, *dressed in a magnificently Victorian tragic robe.*

SLAVE: " Who is't? "

DIKAIOPOLIS:

   " Is thy master there within? "

SLAVE: " Good sir, pray list
   Me here a moment : he's both here and not
   Here ! "

DIKAIOPOLIS *aside:*

         " Here and not here? How, I wonder?
                              (*to* SLAVE) What

   Dost mean? "

SLAVE: " I mean e'en thus : my master's mind
   Is roving forth abroad, in search to find
   Some nifty tragic fancies. But my lord
   Himself is here, upstairs upon the throne—
   In short, writing a tragedy ! "

DIKAIOPOLIS *aside:* The lucky man ! Even his slave's a
   philosopher ! (*to the* SLAVE) Come on, then, call him
   down here for me !

SLAVE: Sir, I can't.

DIKAIOPOLIS: Sir, you'd better, unless you want me
   to batter the door down !

   The SLAVE *stalks inside at this, and slams the door.*
   DIKAIOPOLIS *knocks again.*

Euripides ! Eu-ry !

"Be gracious: no one needs thee more than me—
'Tis I, Dikaiopolis, that's calling thee!"
Yoo-hoo! Eu-ry!

EURIPIDES *sticks his head out of the upstairs window.*

EURIPIDES: I'm busy.

DIKAIOPOLIS: Won't you come down?

EURIPIDES: I can't.

DIKAIOPOLIS: Why not?

EURIPIDES: Don't ask: I just can't!

DIKAIOPOLIS: Well, I'll get the stagehands to move the front of the house away, so that I can speak to you without you moving. Will that do?

EURIPIDES: But—

DIKAIOPOLIS: Come on, don't waste time arguing!

EURIPIDES *resignedly:* Oh, all right! But I don't like the idea one bit!

DIKAIOPOLIS *signs to two* STAGEHANDS, *who revolve the scenery forming the front of the house.* EURIPIDES *is revealed, on the flat roof of the stage building, sitting in a Victorian hip-bath, and sponging himself with a large loofah. His* SLAVE *is sitting beside him, with a notebook ready to take dictation whenever the poet feels inspired.*

DIKAIOPOLIS: Good Heavens! I say, Euripides . . .

EURIPIDES *crossly:* What now?

DIKAIOPOLIS: Whatever are you doing?

EURIPIDES: What does it look like? I'm writing a play!

DIKAIOPOLIS: In the *bath*? Don't your ideas get a little wet?

119

EURIPIDES: Stop trying to be funny, and tell me what you want: it's cold up here!

DIKAIOPOLIS: I only want to borrow one of your tragic costumes for an hour or so—you know, one of the really torn and ragged ones you keep for your grimmest dramas!

EURIPIDES: But why? You're not a tragic actor, are you? I don't believe you could speak a line of tragedy to save your life!

DIKAIOPOLIS: But that's exactly what I've got to do!

He strikes a pose, and declaims:

" It nought avails but I must soon address
Th' Acharnians—and if, in my distress,
I speak th' oration badly, then I die ! "

EURIPIDES:
"Well, which wouldst borrow? Wouldst thou like to try
The robes of Oedipus, in which that man
Did play his saddest part? "

DIKAIOPOLIS:
                    " No, sadder than
Great Oedipus, if thou'd'st be really kind ! "

EURIPIDES:
" Tiresias, then, agèd, helpless and blind? "

DIKAIOPOLIS:
" Not him, no: someone even sadder still ! "

EURIPIDES:
" Who then, good sir? Whatever is thy will?
Wilt have Antigone's torn and dusty clothes? "

DIKAIOPOLIS:
"No, no: far, far more beggarly than those ! "

EURIPIDES:

"I know the man thou want'st! A man whose fate
Was miserable, but whose tongue was really great
At arguing!"

DIKAIOPOLIS: "Yes, that's the sort I crave!"

EURIPIDES:

"I've got the very things! Slave, slave!
Give him the rags King Telephos once wore:
They're there, on top of Haemon's—by the door,
Mix'd up with Creon's"—

The SLAVE rummages through a large pile of filthy-looking rags, and eventually picks some out and throws them down to DIKAIOPOLIS.

SLAVE: "There thou art, good sir!"

DIKAIOPOLIS:

"Now, just one thing more I need: a hat of fur
To match these tragic weeds—"

The SLAVE throws down a hat.

SLAVE: "And there thou art!"

DIKAIOPOLIS begins to go, then turns pensively back.

DIKAIOPOLIS:

"And yet, methinks, before I do depart—"

EURIPIDES *who is getting annoyed:*

"What now? What else wouldst have? A pair of socks?"

DIKAIOPOLIS:

"No, no. I fain would have a wicker box!"

EURIPIDES:

"What need, good sir, for wickerwork?"

DIKAIOPOLIS: "No *need*

To have it: just desire!"

EURIPIDES *throws down a wicker box.*

EURIPIDES *angrily:*   "Here! Sate thy greed

With this, and leave my house with all god-speed!

Depart me hence, I beg!"

DIKAIOPOLIS: "When thou dost make

Me a present of a small, chipp'd cup—"

EURIPIDES: "Here! Take

This one, and go! Thou giv'st me a headache!"

DIKAIOPOLIS:

"I swear I meant not so! But I must ask

One favour more of thee: a little flask

Cork'd up and stopper'd with a sponge!"

EURIPIDES *clutches his forehead, the classic ham gesture of despair.*

EURIPIDES: "Good lord,

I'm ruined! My tragedies cannot afford

To lose another item! Take this, and go!"

DIKAIOPOLIS:

"My friend, thou ask'st me now to leave: but no!

I must demand one simple favour more before—"

EURIPIDES:

"'Tis quite enough! Slave, slave! Close me the door!"

The SLAVE *tries to close the door, then remembers*

that it has been moved aside by the STAGEHANDS. *With some difficulty the scenery is replaced, and he slams the door—an operation that is watched with amusement by* DIKAIOPOLIS. *Now* DIKAIOPOLIS *begins putting on the rags, talking confidentially to the audience as he does so.*

DIKAIOPOLIS: Well, I never thought I'd get as much out of him as that! These playwrights are a stingy lot, at the best of times! Now at least I shall be able to make my defence to the Acharnians in proper style.

He beckons to the CHORUS.

All right, gentlemen: I'm ready.

CHORUS: What is he going to do?
               What is he going to say?
           He's a rogue: he's quite brazen
               Enough to come forward today
           And offer his neck to the city, it's true—
           But he's going to speak, and to reason
               And argue the opposite way
           From the rest of us—yes, even *you*!—
           Without trembling at treason
       As shameless as that! Well sir, come on, then: seek
       To persuade us, as you yourself chose! Come on, speak!

DIKAIOPOLIS' *great speech, the most serious thing in the play, and the moment when Aristophanes openly criticises the way the war is being handled, is made with the noose of the gallows symbolically round his neck. He is dressed by now in the costume of King Telephos, a mythical King who also depended on skilful oratory to get him out of a very unpleasant situation.*

DIKAIOPOLIS: Ladies and gentlemen, don't be annoyed at having to listen to a serious speech in the middle of a comedy. For writers of comedy can distinguish right and wrong as well as anyone else—and, what's more, they're not afraid to speak out, however painful the things they have to say.

You all hate the Spartans—and rightly so: they're the city's enemies. And I hate them, too: I wouldn't trust a Spartan as far as I could throw him, and I pray to the Gods every night to cut down their vines, and ruin their fields, just as they did mine. But don't let's take our hatred of Sparta too far, ladies and gentlemen: there's no sense in blaming them for *everything* that goes wrong, just because they're the enemy!

No: there are some things wrong with Athens that have nothing at all to do with the Spartans. Look around you in the city—can't you see the false treacherous rogues, the counterfeits, who rule Athens now? Can't you see how they go around snapping up all the good things from the shops, confiscating anything that catches their eye, and giving nothing in return? Can't you see how they terrorise the citizens, how no one dares to speak openly, in case one of these men reports him to the officials as a sympathiser with the enemy? Can't you see how they're letting the city slowly bleed to death, while they feather their own nests at your expense?

Consider how the war started in the first place. It all began in Megara. Some of our fine young men got tired of squeezing Athens dry, and decided to turn their attention somewhere else. So, one night, in a drunken frolic, they went off to Megara and captured one of their leading citizens—and when the Megarians complained to us, our noble leaders accused them of treachery, and confiscated all they owned. Naturally, the next thing the Megarians did was to appeal for help to Sparta—which gave the Spartans just the excuse they'd been waiting for. Before we could turn round the two cities were at war, and everywhere you looked there were soldiers.

Whose fault was this? The Spartans'? I don't think so. Suppose it had been the Spartans who'd oppressed Megara, and the Megarians had come to *you* for help— would you have refused? Of course not: you'd have rushed out to attack Sparta, and "right your allies' wrongs". You can't blame the Spartans for doing the same! So whose fault was it? I say it was the fault of those who started the whole business: the fault of these parasites in the city's flesh, these idle and corrupt young men, whose only concerns are to look after their own skins and fill their own pockets, even if it means that every-one else must starve to death, or be captured and enslaved by Sparta. And whose fault is it that they're *allowed* to do this? Don't tell me the Spartans are to blame for that! No—*we're* to blame, all of us: we should have risen against them long ago, and shown them who was master!

Pause.

DIKASTES *thoughtfully:* He's right, you know, quite right—

POLYPRAGMON: Right? How dare he speak like that? Of course he isn't right! He's a traitor—and anyone who agrees with him is a traitor too!

DIKASTES: No, I don't agree: what he's said is the truth—

POLYPRAGMON: Oh, you think it's the truth, do you? (*grimly*) Well, I don't, and I'm not letting him get away with it! He's not going to talk like that while I'm around!

He draws his sword and makes for DIKAIOPOLIS.

DIKASTES: Oh no you don't! Anyone attacking Dikaiopolis has *me* to reckon with as well!

He, too, draws his sword, and a short duel ensues: after a while POLYPRAGMON, *who is getting the worst of it, calls despairingly:*

POLYPRAGMON: Help! Lamachos, help! Your enemies are defeating us! Come out and defend us! Help!

There is a roar from behind the scenes, the door of LAMACHOS' *house is flung open, and* LAMACHOS *himself comes out, brandishing an enormous sword. He is dressed in shining armour, carries a shield with a huge Gorgon's head painted on it, and the plumes on his helmet are about three feet high.*

LAMACHOS *exaggeratedly:*

"Whence came the warcry? Whither shall my aid
Go flying? Where shall tumult rise? Who woke
My shield-encrusted Gorgon from repose?"

DIKAIOPOLIS *aside:* Oh lord, here's one of them! Just the kind of man I meant! All talk and no action—Lamachos the almighty hero!

POLYPRAGMON: Lamachos, my lord! Save us! This traitor here has been slandering our noble leaders!

LAMACHOS:

"And thou, a beggar, dar'st to speak like this?"

DIKAIOPOLIS *pretends to be terrified.*

DIKAIOPOLIS: Oh Lamachos, great hero . . . d-d-don't hit me! I'm s-sorry! Please forgive me!

LAMACHOS *pleased with this result:* But what did you say to them? (*encouragingly*) Don't be afraid: you'll get a fair trial—before we find you guilty! Come on, what was it you said?

DIKAIOPOLIS: I . . . I can't remember! I g-g-go all petrified with fright whenever I catch sight of w-weapons! Please stop pointing that G-g-gorgon at me!

LAMACHOS *magnanimously:* There.

DIKAIOPOLIS *is thoroughly enjoying himself, as* LAMACHOS *becomes more and more mystified by what follows.*

DIKAIOPOLIS: No, no: put it face downwards, here in front of me. Thank you. Now, please give me a feather out of your plume.

LAMACHOS: There you are. Now what?

DIKAIOPOLIS *triumphantly:* Now, will you please hold my head for me? I want to be sick!

He pretends to be sick into the upturned shield.

LAMACHOS *furiously:* What? How dare you use my plumes to make yourself sick! That feather came off a—

DIKAIOPOLIS: Great Crested Brag?

LAMACHOS *spluttering with rage:* W-wha-what? That did it! You've had it now!

DIKAIOPOLIS *in feigned terror:* No, please don't kill me! You know how people hate violence in the theatre!

LAMACHOS: Hmmph!

DIKAIOPOLIS: I tell you what, though—

LAMACHOS: What?

DIKAIOPOLIS: If you really *want* to use that sharp sword and that monster of a shield, you could—

LAMACHOS *fiercely:* Yes? What?

DIKAIOPOLIS: You could give me a haircut!

LAMACHOS *beside himself with rage:* You . . . you . . . you! A beggar speaking like that to a general! How dare you?

DIKAIOPOLIS: Me, a beggar?

LAMACHOS: Well, aren't you?

DIKAIOPOLIS: No: I'm an honest, upright citizen— which is more than can be said for you!

LAMACHOS: What do you mean? I'm a general: I was lawfully elected—

DIKAIOPOLIS: Yes—by a trio of cuckoos! When have you ever done any *fighting*? What have you *ever* done to deserve your title of 'general', except draw your pay every Friday, and put on fancy dress every time you leave the house?

LAMACHOS: By democracy, am I to endure this slander?

DIKAIOPOLIS: You would if you thought you'd be well paid for it!

LAMACHOS: H'm! So you think I never do any fighting? I'll show you! I'll go to Megara, and give *them* what-for! I'll beat the living daylights out of them, and chop them into little pieces—that'll show you whether I ever fight or not!

He starts gathering his equipment for a grand exit.

DIKAIOPOLIS: You'll never even get there! Windbag! I proclaim to all the citizens of Greece—Spartans, Athenians, Megarians, Boeotians, everyone—that this afternoon

I'm opening a free market, here, outside my house—a free-trade area that anyone can come and join, whatever their politics!

LAMACHOS: Hmmmph!

DIKAIOPOLIS: Hmmmph!

They stalk off in opposite directions.

DIKASTES: So much for that! A fat lot of use Lamachos was to *you*!

POLYPRAGMON: You can laugh! But I still think he's a fine general!

DIKASTES: Well, there's no time to argue—we've got the Parabasis to do! Tell them to let Lakrateides go: there's no need to keep him prisoner, now that the speech is over!

LAKRATEIDES is fetched from DIKAIOPOLIS' house, and the CHORUS prepare for the Parabasis.

Ready, gentlemen? We'll start off, and you join in when we come to the chorus part. Right? Off you go, then, Polypragmon: one, two, three—

POLYPRAGMON:

For two or three years now our poet has been
    Coming forward before you, and putting on plays
Here in Athens: but in those years you've never seen
    Him indulging in boasting, or flattery, or praise
Of himself. But he knows how his enemies try
    To revile him and harm him, how fickle the minds
Of the citizens are, how they take any lie
    For the truth if it's plausibly spoken.

LAKRATEIDES:

                          All kinds

Of false stories have been spread abroad: that he mocks
　　At our city, and laughs in its face. So he wants
To attempt, now, to answer these charges: he talks
　　Of regaining your confidence; loudly he flaunts
(Since he has to) the numerous ways that he's tried
　　To help Athens. So, if you're no longer deceived
By plausible strangers who flatter your pride
　　And then cheat you, and if now *at last* you've
　　　achieved
Some success in your public affairs, it's all due
　　To our eminent author, whose glorious name
Makes our allies bring tribute, and come to behold
　　The one poet who's truthful.

DIKASTES:

　　　　　　　　　　　　All this made his name
And his courage notorious—so much so, we're told,
　　That the Great King in Persia, soon after he'd asked
Some envoys of Sparta to tell him which town
　　Had the best and most prosperous fleet at once
　　　passed
To this question: "This poet of such great renown,
　　Is it Athens he satires, or Sparta? For whichever
It is will be prosp'rous if only they heed
　　What he says: if they listen to him they will never
Be beaten in battle—their poet will lead
　　Them to victory!"

POLYPRAGMON:

　　　　　　　　　　　Our author will stay here, and let
Poor old Cleon attempt

　　　　　　　　　　　To defeat him, and get
Only scorn and contempt

　　　　　　　　　　　For his tricks. For he knows

130

That what's right and what's just
                            Are his allies—and those
Are allies he can trust,
                            Unlike Cleon's low wiles:
Cowardice, lies,
False pleading, stage sighs,
                            All that cheats and beguiles!
CHORUS: Come to us, Muse of Acharnai, bright-burning
            and blazing like fire,
      That will set Greece aflame, that will rouse us, and
            quickly inspire
        Us to listen, to hark
      To true wisdom wherever it's found!
      Let our great poet's name resound
      Till everyone knows it! Please, Muse, come and join us,
            and lead
        Us away from the cruelty and limitless dark
      Brought by War: come down to us, Muse, in our hour
            of great need!

*

SCENE THREE

*Scene: the same. A large market-stall, covered with all
sorts of provisions, has been set up outside* DIKAIO-
POLIS' *front door. He comes out carrying a trumpet, and
sounds a fanfare.*

DIKAIOPOLIS: I declare the International Market open!
Peloponnesians, Spartans, Boeotians, Megarians, Thebans

—anyone may come and trade here, providing they trade with me, and not with Lamachos! Entry to the market is forbidden to all spies and informers, and I appoint these whips as market officials, to make sure my instructions are carried out. Now, where's the poster? It's essential to advertise properly!

He goes into his house, just as a MEGARIAN *(Scots accent) comes in, looking half-starved. He carries a large empty sack, and is followed by his two* DAUGHTERS.

MEGARIAN: Ah, here's the market at last! I thought we'd *never* find it! Open to Megarians, too—the only one in the whole of Greece! (*to his* DAUGHTERS) Now then, my wee ones, what d'you say? Are you prepared to go ahead with our plan? Will you do it? Will you let me sell you for food?

DAUGHTERS: Yes, yes!

MEGARIAN: Aye, it's a sad day when a man has to sell his own daughters to get food for the rest of the family! But we've no choice: either you go, or all your brothers and sisters starve! You must pretend to be piglets, and get inside the sack—and I hope your new master's better able to feed you than your father was! Here, now: put on these hooves and these cardboard snouts, and get into the sack, while I call Dikaiopolis.

The DAUGHTERS *dress up as piglets and climb into the sack, while the* MEGARIAN *goes and knocks at* DIKAIOPOLIS' *door.*

Dikaiopolis!

No answer. He turns back to the children, who are now hidden inside the sack.

Now be sure and grunt properly when I tell you! otherwise we'll never get you sold!

He turns back to the house.

Dikaiopolis! Dikaiopolis! D'you want to purchase a pair of piglets?

DIKAIOPOLIS *comes out of the house.*

DIKAIOPOLIS: Did somebody call me? Oh, it's a Megarian! Welcome to the market, my friend. How are things in Megara?

MEGARIAN: Oh, not so good, not so good. We're being half-starved by the Athenian garrison: nothing to eat but what they leave!

DIKAIOPOLIS: What about the famous Megarian garlic fields?

MEGARIAN: Ruined! They go out and dig up the young shoots, just for spite! It never gets a chance to grow!

DIKAIOPOLIS: And you've come here to do business with me? What have you brought me?

MEGARIAN: Are you interested in a brace of piglets?

DIKAIOPOLIS: Piglets?

MEGARIAN: Aye, for the sacrifice.

DIKAIOPOLIS: What're they like? May I see them?

MEGARIAN: Here: just put your hand in the sack, and you can feel their snouts.

DIKAIOPOLIS *rummages in the sack, then suddenly stops in alarm.*

DIKAIOPOLIS: Here! What sort of piglet is this? It doesn't feel like a snout to me!

At this the MEGARIAN *pretends to be offended.*

133

MEGARIAN: What d'you mean, what sort of piglet is it? It's a proper, ordinary little piglet—I raised it myself!

DIKAIOPOLIS: Well, it doesn't feel like one to me.

MEGARIAN: Perhaps you'd like to hear them grunting? Would that convince you?

DIKAIOPOLIS: Yes: let's hear them grunting.

MEGARIAN *to the sack:* Come on, then: grunt!

Silence.

Grunt, damn you!

Silence. He kicks the sack and shouts despairingly:

D'you want me to take you home again—*hungry?*

At this the DAUGHTERS *begin to grunt frenziedly.*

DAUGHTERS: Oink! Oink-oink!

MEGARIAN: There you are! Sound like piglets now, don't they?

DIKAIOPOLIS *doubtfully:* I suppose so. How much do you want for them?

MEGARIAN: A bundle of garlic, and a pound of salt!

DIKAIOPOLIS: That seems fair enough.

He fetches the goods and gives them to the MEGARIAN. *Suddenly however, he is struck by another thought:*

Just a minute, though: what do they eat?

MEGARIAN: Why don't you ask them yourself?

DIKAIOPOLIS: All right. (*to the sack*) Here, piglets, what would you like for supper? Figs? Cheese? Kitchen scraps?

DAUGHTERS: Oink-oink!

DIKAIOPOLIS: I see! What about some juicy roast pork?

In their eagerness, the DAUGHTERS *forget they are supposed to be piglets.*

DAUGHTERS: Ooh! Yes please! Yes, yes please!

DIKAIOPOLIS: I thought so! Piglets, indeed! (*with pity*) Things are as bad as that, are they?

MEGARIAN *miserably:* Aye, we're desperate.

DIKAIOPOLIS: Well, I tell you what: take your daughters home, and take this sack of flour as well, with my compliments: I won't stand by and watch innocent people starve!

He gives the MEGARIAN *a sack of flour; the* DAUGHTERS *climb eagerly out of their sack, and they all prepare to leave. But just at this moment* NIKARCHOS, *a government informer, who makes his living spying on others, bustles in.*

NIKARCHOS *roughly:* You there! Where are you from?

MEGARIAN: I'm a pig-merchant from Megara.

NIKARCHOS: From *Megara?* I see! I'll have to report this to the proper authorities!

MEGARIAN *miserably, to* DIKAIOPOLIS: There you are —and it's like this in Megara too!

NIKARCHOS has been thinking up a pun.

NIKARCHOS: You'll be a *valetudinarian* Megarian by the time I've finished with you!

Nobody else laughs, and he loses his temper.

Put down that sack of flour, and come with me! Traitor!

MEGARIAN: Help! Dikaiopolis, help!

DIKAIOPOLIS, who has disappeared behind his stall, comes back with the whips.

DIKAIOPOLIS: This looks like a case for the market-officials! (*to the whips*) How do you find him? Guilty? Good! I'll see to the punishment!

He starts to beat NIKARCHOS.

NIKARCHOS: Stop, stop! I'll have to report this!

DIKAIOPOLIS: Go on, then: and while you're at it, report *this* as well!

He redoubles the blows, and NIKARCHOS *runs out.*

Well, there you are, my friend: I don't think you need worry about *him* any more. Off you go, back to Megara!

They shake hands.

MEGARIAN: Goodbye, my friend. And may God bless you for helping us!

He goes out with his DAUGHTERS. DIKAIOPOLIS *busies himself behind the stall.*

CHORUS: There's a happy man! You've seen
How very happily his simple scheme
Has worked out, and how all the cream
    Of the countryside will come
    And bargain with him—everyone
Much happier than they've ever been!

As they finish, a most villainous march can be heard in the distance. It comes nearer and nearer, until a weird procession makes its way on to the stage: first, a BOEOTIAN *spiv (Cockney accent), a wide boy eager to do business wherever he smells a chance of profit; he is followed by a ragged, snivelling slave,* ISMENIAS, *loaded with baskets, and finally a group of hack* MUSICIANS, *piping inexpertly at a third-rate tune.*

BOEOTIAN: Phew! Hercules, but I'm exhausted! It's all this merchandise I'm carrying!

He is, of course, carrying nothing.

Ismenias, lad, that's right: put the stuff down there—carefully, though: we don't want the pennyroyal crushed, now do we? And you other lads, stop this march now. How about a chorus of my favourite melody—*(expansively)*—"The Dawg's Behind"?

The MUSICIANS strike up an even more vulgar tune, which brings DIKAIOPOLIS out from behind his stall with a rush.

DIKAIOPOLIS: Stop, stop, for Heaven's sake! Clear off! What a crowd of wasps! What a swarm of wheezing bagpipers! Shoo—and don't hurry back!

He chases the MUSICIANS away. The BOEOTIAN, seeing his reaction to the music, now changes his own tune to fit.

BOEOTIAN: Cor, thanks a lot: that was a real favour! I've been trying to get rid of them, all the way from Thebes! *(sententiously)* Of course, I only go in for Classical Music myself—can't stand this popular rubbish!

DIKAIOPOLIS: H'm. And what brings *you* here?

BOEOTIAN *confidentially—this is sales-talk:* I've got some very choice items here for the discriminating shopper—very choice indeed, though I say so myself! Here's a nice line: chickens, plump and ready for the oven. I can let you have them at a knock-down price—as a purely personal favour, mind! I wouldn't like the word to get around . . .

DIKAIOPOLIS *doubtfully:* Ye-es. Anything else?

BOEOTIAN: Anything else, he asks me! Look at these—all good-selling, bargain items, I promise you—marjoram, pennyroyal, lamp-wicks, ducklings, jackdaws, woodcocks, marsh-hens, running-birds, kingfishers: you name it, we've got it!

DIKAIOPOLIS *sarcastically:* The early worm catches the bird, I suppose!

BOEOTIAN *in an aggrieved tone:* I hadn't finished, had I? (*in his selling voice*) Foxes, hedge-hogs, lyres, moles, voles, coconut matting, cats, martens, fine Copaic eels—

DIKAIOPOLIS: Stop! Copaic eels, did you say? They're my favourite food! Let's see them!

The BOEOTIAN *takes a jar of eels from one of the baskets, and holds it up to admire it.*

BOEOTIAN: Come along, you little darlings, then! Fine and sleek, aren't you? Sweet enough for a King's table! (*confidentially, to* DIKAIOPOLIS) I can let you have these at a knock-down price—as a purely per—

DIKAIOPOLIS: Never mind the price, I'll take them! What d'you want for them? Cash down, or some local goods in exchange?

BOEOTIAN: Such as what?

DIKAIOPOLIS: Athenian anchovies? Or best-quality china pots?

BOEOTIAN *with mock surprise:* Anchovies or pots? Do me a favour! I want something *unusual*—something you have here that we haven't got at home! Anchovies! Pots! I should coco!

Suddenly a CITIZEN *rushes in, terrified, and cowers down by* DIKAIOPOLIS' *stall.* NIKARCHOS *stalks after him, and begins taking down his name and address in a black notebook.*

DIKAIOPOLIS: I've got the very thing! What about an *informer?*

BOEOTIAN: What's one of them?

DIKAIOPOLIS: There's one, over there.

BOEOTIAN *dubiously:* He's a bit small, isn't he?

DIKAIOPOLIS: Small, but deadly.

BOEOTIAN: But what's he good for?

DIKAIOPOLIS: Anything: thieving, lying, beating people up, spying, informing—whatever you want from him!

NIKARCHOS: Somebody want me?

He sees the BOEOTIAN.

Oh! I'll have to report *you* to the authorities, you know!

BOEOTIAN: Me? What have I done?

NIKARCHOS: You've imported hostile lamp-wicks!

DIKAIOPOLIS *aside to the BOEOTIAN:* See what I mean?

NIKARCHOS goes and starts taking down details of the BOEOTIAN's baskets, not realising the bargaining that is going on behind his back.

BOEOTIAN: Cor! Is he like that all the time?

DIKAIOPOLIS: He never stops.

BOEOTIAN: I could be famous! I could make myself his manager—suppose I put him in a cage, and charged people a penny a time to let him take their particulars? (*eagerly*) I'll have him! What d'you want for him?

DIKAIOPOLIS: Suppose we do a swop? You take him, and I'll take charge of what you brought with you!

139

BOEOTIAN: Done! You've got yourself a bargain!

He signs to ISMENIAS *and* XANTHIAS, *who pounce on* NIKARCHOS, *and began tying him up.*

NIKARCHOS: Help, help! I denounce—

A gag, efficiently inserted into his mouth, cuts him off in mid-whine.

DIKAIOPOLIS: Wrap him up carefully, now: we don't want him broken in transit! That's right! Now, roll him up in this carpet!

NIKARCHOS *is rolled up inside an old piece of carpet, and piled on to* ISMENIAS' *reluctant back.*

There you are, my friend, all yours!

BOEOTIAN: Cor, thank you! (*to himself*) What a bargain! I'll make a fortune out of him! What a stroke of luck!

He goes out, with ISMENIAS *and the parcelled-up* NIKARCHOS. *While* DIKAIOPOLIS *is sorting out the contents of the baskets, the* CHORUS *sing a short ode.*

CHORUS:

> Look, my friends, how wise and clever this man is:
>   For, now that he's made peace,
> He decides at once to give the State a miss,
>   And sits here at his ease,
> Buying and selling the sort of goods not seen
> In Athens since the war began—oh yes: he's been
>   Wiser than any of us, and he's
> The man to rescue us, to help when times are lean!

*

SCENE FOUR

Scene: the same. As the C H O R U S finish, the H E R A L D comes in, preceded by a T R U M P E T E R, who blows a fanfare. The H E R A L D then reads a proclamation.

H E R A L D: Oyez, oyez! By order of the Peace Tribunal! All men who wish to enter for the drinking contest must, at the sound of the trumpet, drain their goblets. The man who's first to empty his, will win a cask of best red wine!

His proclamation over, he looks around, as though trying to find something, then goes up to D I K A I O P O L I S.

Excuse me, sir: can you tell me where General Lamachos lives? I know it's in this street somewhere.

D I K A I O P O L I S: Yes, that's right: it's over there.

The H E R A L D goes and knocks loudly on L A M A - C H O S' door.

H E R A L D: Great Lamachos! O bullshide-shielded lord! Gorgon-bearer! Helmet-wobbler! Lamachos, come forth!

L A M A C H O S pokes his head out of the window.

L A M A C H O S: "Who knocketh at my brass-bound dwelling-place?"

H E R A L D: The officials send you word that you're to go, at once, and take up garrison duty on the frontiers: word has come that the Boeotians are planning to invade from Thrace, under cover of the snow!

L A M A C H O S: "Alack! O woe! To have to stand about in snow!"

He withdraws his head and closes the window. The

HERALD turns and points dramatically at DIKAIO-POLIS.

HERALD *in a voice like the crack of doom:* Dikaiopolis!
DIKAIOPOLIS *aside:* Oh lord, not me as well! I can't stand snow! (*to the* HERALD) Yes, what is it?
HERALD: The priest of Dionysos orders you, now, at once, to go and take up duty as his guest: he's giving a feast in honour of Peace, and commands you to bring your treaty-bottle and your wine-jug, and go to dinner!

He and the TRUMPETER *go out.* LAMACHOS *comes out of his house.*

LAMACHOS: " Woe is me! "
DIKAIOPOLIS: What's wrong?
LAMACHOS: " 'Tis cold, yea, cold, the chilling snow! "
DIKAIOPOLIS: Can't you wrap yourself up in your Gorgon, and keep warm that way?

LAMACHOS turns dramatically to call his SLAVE.

LAMACHOS:
　　" Slave, slave! My army knapsack! Bring it forth! "
DIKAIOPOLIS:
　　" Slave, slave! My banquet clothing! Bring it forth! "

Lamachos' SLAVE *and* XANTHIAS *come out, and begin preparing their masters for departure.*

LAMACHOS:
　　" My helmet-plumes! Attach them carefully! "
DIKAIOPOLIS:
　　" My olive crown! Attach it carefully! "
LAMACHOS:
　　" How fine and fair this Gorgon gleameth! "

DIKAIOPOLIS:

"How tenderly-cooked this turkey seemeth!"

LAMACHOS *angrily:*

"Sir, from this mocking of my arms desist!"

DIKAIOPOLIS:

"Sir, from this drooling o'er my food leave off!"

LAMACHOS *to his* SLAVE:

"Fetch me out here my triple-crest-plate-ridge!"

DIKAIOPOLIS *to* XANTHIAS:

"Fetch me out here my fine-curved knife and fork!"

LAMACHOS *examines his helmet with dismay.*

LAMACHOS:

"Alack! The moth has gnawed away my plume!"

DIKAIOPOLIS:

"Alack! I fear for the food I won't have room!"

LAMACHOS:

"Sir, kindly do not dare to mock at me!

Slave, slave! Unhook and hither bring my spear!"

DIKAIOPOLIS:

"Slave, slave! Unhook and bring my sausage here!"

LAMACHOS:

"Oil well the buckler, slave! Hah! What see I?

I see an old fool charged with cowardice!"

DIKAIOPOLIS:

"Oil well the frying pan, slave! Hah! What see I?

I see 'an old fool' mocking Lamachos—

The Gorgon-mothered weeps in helpless rage!"

LAMACHOS:

"Slave, slave! My thickest armour-plating bring!"

DIKAIOPOLIS:

"Slave, slave! My widest drinking-goblet bring!"

LAMACHOS:

"With this I may avail to down the foe!"

DIKAIOPOLIS:

"With this I may avail to down my drink!"

LAMACHOS:

"Pick up the shield, and let's begone!"

He stalks out, then runs back hurriedly, exclaiming in a normal voice:

Phew! It's snowing! What a chilly business!

He puts up a large umbrella, with some difficulty because of his helmet-plumes, and goes off again.

DIKAIOPOLIS: Come on, Xanthias: my business is warmer!

He goes off triumphantly in the opposite direction.

CHORUS:

Go forward rejoicing, and ready to thrive
    In your quite different, quite separate ways:
One to be crowned, and to drink, and to wive,
    And to bask in the glory of well-deserved praise;
The other to shiver, and cower down, and freeze
    As the snow whirls about him, and eagerly makes
His ironmongery chill to the touch, while the breeze
    Whips his cheeks, and he shivers and shakes.
The moral's quite clear: when a man looks for peace,
    He is happy and honoured, and lives at his ease—
But a man who is eager for nothing but war
    Must find suffering as no one has suffered before!
This is the point of our play—and if *you*
    Prefer war, after this, you'll very soon see

That it's true: as the snow turns you blue
    You'll be wishing—too late—that you'd listened to
    me!

*At this point Lamachos' S L A V E rushes in, in a frenzy
of mock-heroics. He imagines he is delivering the Messenger's speech in a tragedy, and declaims accordingly:*

S L A V E :
    " Ye slaves within the house of Lamachos,
      Warm well some water in an earthen pot;
    Prepare him ointments, and bring linen cloths
      And greasy wool and bandage for his foot!
    The master hurt his ankle on a wooden stake
      The whiles he leapt across a trenchèd moat;
    And as he leapt the other way, he brake
      His leg in twain, and eke his nut he smote
    Quite sorely on a marbled rock; and then
    His braggart plume fell ragged down—and when
    Our lord did see that sight, then did he yield
      Himself to tragic passiòn, and cried:
    ' O star' (quotha), 'O radiant buckler'd eye,
      Now is the final time I'll thee have spied,
    For now both thou, and I thy lord, shall die!'
      Thus speaking, straight he fell into a pond,
    But, leaping out again, pursu'd a band
      Of robbers, riding on despite his wound!
    Open! He comes! Come forth and lend a hand!"

Tucket without. L A M A C H O S *is borne in on a
stretcher, very much the worse for wear. He is laid on the
ground, where he rolls about in great distress.*

L A M A C H O S :
    "Ye Gods! Ye Gods enthroned on high!

What agony! What have ye done to me?
I'm ruined! Woe is me, alas—
The foe has worsted me, oh lack-a-day!"

He adds, in a ham aside to the audience:

That was very good, I thought: thank goodness Dikaiopolis isn't around, to spoil my big scene!

But his hopes are shattered: for, as if on cue,
DIKAIOPOLIS *now comes in, with a dancing-girl on each arm, and obviously thoroughly enjoying himself.*

DIKAIOPOLIS:
"Ye Gods! Ye Gods enthroned on high!
What beauties! What a pair of birdlets!
I'm ruined! Woe is me, alas—
I'll never kiss them both at once!"

LAMACHOS *makes a gallant rearguard attempt to win the word-battle.*

LAMACHOS:
"O blow so fatal, so unjust! O fate!
O cruel painful wounds! Alack, alas!"

DIKAIOPOLIS *in feigned surprise:* Goodness me! It's Lamachos, the Colonel of the Nut Brigade!

LAMACHOS: "O wretched me!"

DIKAIOPOLIS *to one of the girls:* My dear, do you love me?

LAMACHOS: "O mournful I!"

DIKAIOPOLIS *to the other girl:* My dear, will you kiss me?

LAMACHOS: "What a terrible blow has come to pass!"

DIKAIOPOLIS: Yes—it passed me all right: I never even saw it!

LAMACHOS: "My leg! My leg! O take me in!"

DIKAIOPOLIS: "My loves! My loves! O take me in!"

LAMACHOS:
"I'm miserably piercèd to the bone! Alack!
What dreadful pain! I'm ruined! Woe!"

He is borne into his house, to the sound of a funeral march.

DIKAIOPOLIS: I won! I was the first man to empty my wine-cup when the trumpet sounded! I've won the prize!

DIKASTES: And you're the happiest man in Athens!

DIKAIOPOLIS: I won, I won. The prize is mine!

POLYPRAGMON: Let's go inside and celebrate!

There is a gay procession into DIKAIOPOLIS' house, with everyone shouting 'He's won! Hurrah! The prize is his!' etc. DIKAIOPOLIS is left alone on the stage, and comes forward to pronounce the Epilogue, while his dancing-girls wait for him in the doorway of his house.

DIKAIOPOLIS:
Ladies and gentlemen, the play is done;
    But there's one thing more I want to say to you—
This dreadful Spartan war's oppressing everyone,
    And yet, strange though it is, there are very few
Of us who're willing to rouse ourselves and end
    It—why? There isn't any mighty Cause
Left for us to fight for! So why not rise
    Against the crooks and traitors who oppress us?
    Why wait? Why let these scoundrels still distress us?
Don't yield—destroy them! Peace will be the prize!

How can you start, you ask? It's easy—send
Us home rejoicing, warmed by your applause!

He bows, and then goes and joins the dancing-girls, putting his arms round them, and leading them into his house.

*

4

PEACE

NOTE

Peace, though a different kind of play from *The Achar-nians*, makes an excellent foil to it. Both plays are concerned with the efforts of single individuals to bring peace back to Athens; but whereas, in *The Acharnians*, Dikaiopolis is only interested in winning peace for *himself*, Trygaios, in this play, tries to help the whole city—to find a cure, not only for his own afflictions, but for those of all his fellow-citizens as well.

Peace was first put on four years after *The Acharnians*, four years that had passed without any sign that the war was nearing its end. In that time a new class of leaders, even worse than the corrupt generals of *The Acharnians*, had arisen in the city: ruthless demagogues, who swayed the people by the power of their oratory, and cared more for personal advantage than for saving the city. The worst of them all was the ex-tanner Cleon, whose fiery eloquence and misplaced zeal soon persuaded the people that he was the only man who could lead them to victory—and the bitter attacks made on him, in this and other plays, are the only signs that anyone saw through his bluster to the heartless ambition underneath. However, one year before the first production of *Peace*, Cleon made a fatal mistake: he allowed himself to be elected general, the one job where oratory was not enough. He was killed in battle shortly afterwards, and few people mourned him. But even his memory seems to have roused Aristophanes to fury: the vitriolic attacks made on him in the Parabasis of this play (p. 178) are blunter than anything he wrote when Cleon was still alive.

Peace is cynical (particularly about the Gods) and savage;

but it probably very well sums up the feelings of the Athenian people in 421 : they had been cooped up in the city now for over ten years, with insufficient, constantly rationed food, the perpetual fear of plague, and nothing to do but watch the enemy annually destroy their farmlands, just outside the city walls. Their desperate mood is well caught by a play like this, in which even the best comic ideas (like the opening scene, or the idea of War roasting all the Greek states in a huge oven) are treated with a wild, punchdrunk exuberance, with none of the control and discipline of Aristophanes' other plays. *Peace* may lack some of the greatness of *The Acharnians*, but it remains an extraordinary and in some ways terrifying monument to the anguish and despair of a people left without hope.

The play opens as Trygaios' two servants are feeding a giant dung-beetle, which their master believes will save the world. . . .

PEACE

Characters:

Speaking parts:

TRYGAIOS, *an Athenian farmer*
OIKETES ⎫
SLAVE ⎭ *his servants*
PAIDION, *his daughter*
HERMES, *a God*
WAR
QUARREL, *his boy*
HIEROKLES, *a begging priest*
LAMACHOS, *a general*
FIRST MERCHANT
SECOND MERCHANT

CHORUS *of farmers, led by* GEORGOS *and* AUTOURGOS

Non-speaking parts:

PEGASUS, *a dung-beetle*
PEACE, HARVEST *and* HOLIDAY, *three Goddesses*

153

PEACE

SCENE ONE

The scene is the yard of TRYGAIOS' *farm, not far from Athens. At one side of the stage there is a large hut, with a half-door covering the entrance, and looking rather like a dilapidated stable.* OIKETES *hurries in, beckoning off-stage.*

OIKETES: Come on, mate: hurry up! Bring in another of those pies! The beetle's hungry!

The SLAVE *staggers in, bent double under the weight of a huge pie.*

SLAVE: Here you are! You give it him, the ugly brute! And I hope he's satisfied *this* time!

OIKETES *throws the pie into the stable; immediately there is a tremendous noise of snuffling and grunting.*

OIKETES *admiringly:* Well, look at that! Would you believe it! You'd better go and fetch some more—and quickly!

SLAVE: He hasn't eaten it *already*, has he?

OIKETES: Couldn't even wait to chew it! Rolled it into a ball, he did, and down it went, before you could say Euripides! Go on—fetch him some more: and mix up another batch!

SLAVE *in a tragic aside to the audience:*
> "Come up and help me, sirs, or else I think
> Ye'll see me perish hapless in the stink!"—

(Quote: Euripides!)

154

OIKETES: Stop wasting time: he's waiting!

There is a great gobbling noise from the stable.

(*To the beetle*) What? What was that?

More gobbling.

Oh, I see! (*to the* SLAVE) He says not to put so much pastry on them this time: he finds it a little indigestible!

SLAVE: I'm not surprised, considering what's inside it! You won't catch me stealing the juicy bits out of *his* plates, I can tell you!

OIKETES: For Heaven's sake get on with it—go and fetch him some more!

SLAVE: No! I'm going on strike! There was nothing in my contract about having to put up with *his* stink!

OIKETES: Don't argue! Pick up the pail and go!

SLAVE: Pick it up yourself, and go—to Hell! (*to the audience*) Look here, ladies and gentlemen, I don't suppose any of you could tell me where to buy a plugged-up nose? Believe me, it's no picnic, carting about the sort of food *he* likes! A dog or a pig, now: they're no trouble—they'll eat whatever you put in front of them. But not Lord Muck here! Oh no: he sticks his nose in the air, and refuses to touch a single bite, unless I serve him nicely-rounded pies, with " not too much pastry on them, please "—like a flipping duchess!

There is a grunt from the stable.

Now what's he doing? Let's just take a peep . . .

Gingerly he glances over the stable door, then recoils in disgust.

Damn you! Yes, go on: guzzle till you burst! Ugh, the filthy brute! Reminds me of a wrestler, the way he gets them on the floor, and then puts a double jaw-lock on them! You ought to see his footwork—you'd think he was coiling anchor ropes for barges! Phew, the ugly, greedy, nasty-smelling, filthy—

He breaks off suddenly, and turns to OIKETES.

You know what I think?

OIKETES *ironically:* No—what do you think?

SLAVE: I think he's meant to be Cleon, or something, the way he goes mad over dirt and dung like that!

OIKETES: Never mind who he's supposed to be: all *you've* to worry about is keeping him well-fed!

There is a grunt of agreement from the stable.

You see! Go and get him something to drink!

The SLAVE *goes out grumbling, and* OIKETES *turns to the audience.*

I suppose you're wondering what all this is about? Well, I'll tell you the plot so far. (*confidentially*) My master's cracked—round the bend, he is! Not like *you*, though, not mad about war! No, he's caught some strange, new kind of madness. D'you know what he does? He stands there all day long, gazing up at the sky, and shouting: "Hey, Zeus! Zeus up there! What are you playing at? Can't you leave Greece alone for a bit? We've had enough!"

TRYGAIOS *from inside:* O Zeus!

OIKETES: There he is, you see! Just listen to him now!

TRYGAIOS *from inside:* Zeus! Zeus up there! What are you trying to do? There'll be none of us left pretty soon!

156

OIKETES: There you are! Just what I said he said! That's the kind of thing he keeps shouting—at the empty sky, mark you! And that's not all: d'you know what he said when he first went mad? "Well," he said, "And why not go *up* there, and have a word with Zeus in person?" Round the bend! Out he gets a pair of kitchen steps, and starts off up them, trying to get to Heaven. So of course he falls and nearly breaks his neck! *Then* what d'you think he does? He goes off, God knows where, and buys this thoroughbred, Lord Muck here! And I have to groom it, like a flipping horse! All the while he's stroking it, and cuddling it, and saying:

"My Pegasus! My glossy, wingèd steed!
Thou'rt here to help me in my direst need,
And take me up to Zeus with swiftest speed"—

and so on, like a bloke in a tragedy! (*pause*) Here! It's gone very quiet all of a sudden! What's going on? What's he doing?

He peers into the stable.

Oh, good lord! Help, neighbours, help! The master's setting off for Heaven, on the back of his beetle! Help, help!

The stable door is flung wide open, and TRYGAIOS *jogs into the farmyard, riding his huge beetle, which is saddled and bridled like a horse.*

TRYGAIOS:

Quietly, quietly, steady now, Dobbin!
Steady, there, steady now! Calmly, please!
Whoa, boy!

He brings the beetle to a halt, and pats its neck affectionately.

157

OIKETES: Here, master, you must be mad! This stinking—

TRYGAIOS: Shhh! You'll upset him! He's very sensitive, you know!

OIKETES: But, master, why are you riding a *beetle*?

TRYGAIOS: To get to Heaven, of course!

OIKETES: But *why*? What are you going to Heaven for?

TRYGAIOS: I just want to have a quick word with Zeus —I shall say to him, straight out, man to man: "Now look here, Zeus old boy: what's going on? What d'you intend to do to Greece?"—or words to that effect!

OIKETES: Suppose he refuses to listen?

TRYGAIOS: He'd better listen! If he doesn't, I'll have him up in court, for betraying Greece to the enemy!

OIKETES: You're crazy! (*with sudden determination*) I won't have it! If you go, it'll be over my dead body!

He plants himself firmly in front of the beetle.

TRYGAIOS: All right, if that's the way you want it . . .

He starts riding towards him. OIKETES *holds his ground till the very last moment; but his nerve finally breaks, and he jumps clear.*

OIKETES: Oh dear! Help! Paidion, Paidion, come out here quickly! You're losing your father! Going away to Heaven, he is, without so much as saying 'ta-ta!'*

"Come out here now, and with thy tears beguile
Thy sire, poor dear, to tarry yet awhile!"

PAIDION, *Trygaios' daughter, rushes out from the farmhouse in mock-tragic despair, and clings to her father.*

PAIDION:

    " Oh father, dear father, I beg you : don't go !
    The news has just come that you're off ! What a blow
    To your fam'ly to lose you ! We love you, we do !
    Oh pater, I beg you to say it's not true ! "

TRYGAIOS: I'm sorry, my dear, but I've no choice : I
must go. To tell the truth, I'm sick and tired of hearing
my children crying for bread, and not being able to do
anything about it. The only thing I *can* do is try and
find Peace myself—and when I *do* find her, and bring
her back, I promise you'll never go short of food again !

PAIDION:

    ' But what's the route on which thou mean'st to wend
    Thy way? Where shall this frightening journey end?
    No ship there is to take thee, none to send ! "

TRYGAIOS:

    " My wingèd steed shall bear me hence : I need
    No ship, and none demand ! "

PAIDION:

    " But why a steed
    So foul, O sire? A horse with wings would lead
    Thee to the Gods more tragic'lly by far ! "

TRYGAIOS:

    " Thou know'st what greedy eaters horses are ! "

PAIDION:

    " Oh woe is me !
    Suppose thou tumblest in the stormy brine?
    How may thy wingèd bettle save thee? "

TRYGAIOS:

    " Fine !
    I've got some oars in case of that : I'll float
    Him on his back, and use him as a boat ! "

PAIDION:

"But where the port to take thee in, sad sire?"

TRYGAIOS:

"The *beetling* crag of the Piraeus is higher
Than any other: I'll simply aim for there!"

PAIDION:

"Pater, be careful, lest thou fall'st from the air
And break'st thy legs in twain! Thy wounded knees
Would be sad enough for great Euripides
To put in one of his gloomy tragedies!"

*This tragic cross-talk could go on for ever: but
TRYGAIOS suddenly remembers that his mission, after
all, is not a comic one, and becomes more serious:*

TRYGAIOS: Yes, yes, my dear: I'll be as careful as I
can. But you *can* see how essential it is for me to go,
can't you?

PAIDION *sadly:* Yes, father: I suppose so.

TRYGAIOS: Well, goodbye, my child. I'll get back as soon
as I can.

He kisses her farewell, and then turns to the audience.

And all of you: don't forget *you're* the ones I'm trying
to help! Try and hold off from fighting while I'm away—
once I've rescued Peace, there'll never be any need for
war again! (*to the beetle*) Gee up, now, Pegasus—let's see
if you can live up to your name! But no aerobatics,
please—don't forget you've got a passenger!

*He nods to the man operating the crane which will
lift the beetle up in the air.*

O.K.! Chocks away!

The beetle begins slowly to rise in the air. Those in the farmyard wave goodbye, and then go inside. TRY-GAIOS *is hugely enjoying himself—for this is the first time mankind has ever taken to the air.*

This is magnificent! I can see the whole city from here, spread out below me like a map! And how tiny everything looks! There's the harbour, and the Assembly (yes, and they're still arguing, I see!)—oh, and look: over there some soldiers are drilling! How very small they look!

Suddenly the beetle lurches violently, and he turns angrily to the crane-operator.

Here! What's the big idea? Keep your mind on your job! You'll have me off! Don't ruin the whole plot before I even *get* to Heaven!

Without any further mishap the beetle rises until it stops level with the roof of the stage-building.

Ah, but this looks like Heaven now. Whoa, boy!

He climbs off the beetle on to the roof.

Yes, this must be Zeus' door. I'll knock. Hullo inside!

He hammers on the door. There is no reply.

Hullo, I said! Are none of the Gods at home today?

He renews his hammering on the door. Suddenly it opens, and HERMES *rushes furiously out.*

HERMES: Who on earth's doing all this knocking! You'll break the door down!

He catches sight of the beetle, and recoils violently.

Ooh-er! What the devil's *that*?

TRYGAIOS: A flying beetle-horse! Pegasus, to you!

HERMES: My goodness, a mortal man!

Without stopping for breath, he shouts the following catechism at TRYGAIOS:

You dreadful daring nasty man you quite revolting little mortal you horrid nasty scoundrel why've you come and what's your name? (*breath*) What's your name, I said!

TRYGAIOS: Scoundrel! Will that do?

HERMES *ignoring him*: Father's name—if any!

TRYGAIOS: Scoundrel!

HERMES *still ignoring him*: Christian name *and* surname, if you don't mind!

TRYGAIOS: Look, I've told you! Scoundrel, Scoundrel, Scoundrel!

HERMES *draws himself up to his full height.*

HERMES: Sir, are you mocking me—*me* a God? I'll have you thrown into Hell, unless you answer properly! WHAT'S YOUR NAME?

TRYGAIOS: Trygaios, from Athmonia near Athens. I—

HERMES: H'm! So you *are* a mortal! What do you want? Are you dead?

TRYGAIOS: No, I—

HERMES *distastefully*: You're not another of these 'philosophers', are you, come up here to prove that the Gods don't exist?

TRYGAIOS: No, I'm just a simple farmer. I—

HERMES: For goodness' sake don't stand there mumbling! I haven't got all day!

162

Suddenly TRYGAIOS *realises that all* HERMES *wants is the traditional bribe anyone visiting Heaven or Hell is supposed to give the doorkeeper. He fishes a meat sandwich out of his lunch-box.*

TRYGAIOS: Well . . . er . . . actually, I came to bring you this! I know all you get up here's ambrosia, and I thought you might appreciate something a little different for a change!

HERMES, *a God renowned for his gluttony, eagerly accepts the sandwich, and his manner immediately changes.*

HERMES *with his mouth full:* Oh thank you, my mortal friend! Now, what was it you said you wanted?

TRYGAIOS: Mortal friend, indeed! I thought I was a scoundrel! Come on, stop wasting time: call Zeus!

HERMES *amused:* Call Zeus? *(aside to the audience)* That's all they ever want! *(to* TRYGAIOS*)* I'm sorry, but he's not at home! They've all gone away: packed their bags and gone off for a holiday—there's no one here but me!

TRYGAIOS: But where on earth—

HERMES: Just hark at that! On *earth*!

TRYGAIOS: Well, where then?

HERMES: Oh, miles from here! They've gone off to the furthest corner of the sky!

TRYGAIOS: But why *now*, of all times?

HERMES: Because they're fed-up with the Greeks!

TRYGAIOS: What?

HERMES: They're so tired of your squabbling, they've decided to forget about men altogether for a bit, and take a holiday! They've left the God of War behind, hoping he'll clear you Greeks right off the face of the earth by the time they get back!

TRYGAIOS *aghast*: What? You mean they've given us up entirely? But *why*?

HERMES: That's easy: every time they offer you peace in Athens, you shout: "No! We want no part of it! It's a Spartan plot!" And the same thing happens in Sparta: nothing doing!

TRYGAIOS *to the audience*: Yes, it's true enough! That's Cleon, all right!

HERMES: The upshot of it all is, I don't think you'll ever set eyes on Peace again!

TRYGAIOS: Why not? Where's she gone?

HERMES: War's buried her in a hole—

TRYGAIOS: A what?

HERMES: A hole. Down there: look—

He points to a large heap of stones down on the stage.

And that great heap of stones is piled on top, to stop her ever getting out again!

TRYGAIOS: But what's he mean to do with *us*?

HERMES: I don't know much about it—all I can tell you is, that he's just had some new pots and pans delivered, and a huge oven—

TRYGAIOS: An *oven*?

HERMES: Yes: he's talking of making "Greek-city stew", or something!

Suddenly there is a great clattering and banging from behind the stage.

Here! What was that? I think he's coming out! I'm off!

TRYGAIOS: I'm coming with you! That sounded too much like a meat-chopper for comfort!

164

They hurry inside and slam the door. After a few seconds it opens again, and TRYGAIOS *creeps out, whisks the beetle inside with him, and slams the door again.*

*

SCENE TWO

This scene takes place on the stage, which now represents the district of Heaven pointed out from above by HERMES. *The heap of stones is at one side, and a huge oven and a kitchen table covered with various cooking utensils are at the other. The noise of banging and clattering from off-stage grows louder and louder, until* WAR, *a large, heavily-built and fiercely-eyebrowed figure, comes in with another boulder, which he adds to the pile. He then turns to the cooking utensils on the table. Meanwhile* TRYGAIOS *creeps in unobtrusively, and hides himself where he can be seen by the audience, but not by* WAR.

WAR *gloatingly:* O you mortals, you wretched, wretched mortals! You've had it now! There won't be much left of you, by the time I've finished! What a headache *that's* going to be!

TRYGAIOS *aside:* Heavens, what a monster of a frying-pan! And just look at War—so *this* is the God who terrifies us all so much! I certainly wouldn't like to bump into *him* on a dark night!

WAR: You poor Prasians, you poor unhappy Prasians, now you're for it! You'll go nicely in the stew!

He throws some ingredients into a gigantic frying-pan.

TRYGAIOS *aside:* Well, that's all right so far: they're Sparta's allies, not ours!

WAR: And now for you, Megarians!

TRYGAIOS *aside:* Heavens! What a hash he's going to make of Megara!

WAR: And don't you Sicilians imagine *you're* going to escape! You're next!

TRYGAIOS *aside:* H'm! I wouldn't like to be in the Sicilians' shoes right now!

WAR: And now for Athens!

TRYGAIOS *horrified:* No, no! Not the Athenians! They're sour . . . gone off . . . not ripe yet! Don't throw them in! Please!

He cowers down in terror behind the pile of stones. But fortunately WAR is too preoccupied to have heard him. He appears to be looking for something.

WAR: Quarrel! Quarrel! Damn it, where's that boy? *Quarrel!*

QUARREL, WAR's *servant, comes in truculently.*

QUARREL *cheekily:* You called?

WAR: Come on, don't dawdle, or you'll get my fist across your ear!

QUARREL: And what a fist it is!

WAR takes a swing at him.

Ow! Ow! I was only joking! (*aside*) What a stink of garlic!

W A R : What have you done with the matches?

Q U A R R E L *innocently*: Matches? Me? I haven't set eyes on
them!

W A R : Well, where are they, then?

Q U A R R E L : How on earth should I know?

W A R : Don't speak to me like that! Go and buy some, at
the Olympus Stores—hurry!

Q U A R R E L : Sir, you know the shops are shut! The whole
place is closed—all the Gods are on holiday!

W A R : Well, go to Athens, then, and ask Cleon for a box—
he's bound to have some!

Q U A R R E L : But sir—

> W A R *raises his fist threateningly.*

All right, all right! No need to be like that! I'm going!

> *He goes out, making a rude sign at* W A R *behind his
> back.* T R Y G A I O S *turns to the audience.*

T R Y G A I O S : What are we going to do *now*, ladies and
gentlemen? Let's hope he breaks his neck on the way
down—because if he comes back with a box of matches,
we're done for!

> Q U A R R E L *comes back, reluctantly.*

Q U A R R E L : S-s-sir . . .

W A R : Well, what took you so long? And where are the
matches?

Q U A R R E L : S-s-sir, there aren't any!

W A R : What? Didn't you ask Cleon? You know he's a
friend of mine!

Q U A R R E L : I *couldn't* ask him, sir!

W A R : Why not?

QUARREL: He's dead, sir, matches and all—there's nothing left to ask!

TRYGAIOS *aside:* Phew! Thank goodness! That's the first sensible thing Cleon's ever done!

WAR: Well, what are you waiting for? Go to Sparta, and ask Brasidas!

QUARREL: Who?

WAR: Brasidas, you idiot! The chief general! Ask *him* for some—he's a friend of mine as well!

QUARREL: Yes, sir!

He goes out again, and TRYGAIOS *turns once more to the audience.*

TRYGAIOS: That's done it! Things are getting hot! I hope you can remember the prayers they taught you at Sunday-school: if you can't, we're really in trouble!

QUARREL *comes back, even more sheepishly than before.*

QUARREL *miserably:* Oh dear! Oh deary me!

WAR: What's wrong with you now? Snivelling little brat! And where are the matches?

QUARREL *sniffing:* Sir, Brasidas is dead as well! Nff!

WAR: What?

QUARREL: Nff-nfff! Yes, sir! (Nfff!) He went to lend his matches to someone up Thrace-way—(nfff!)—and then he took and shuffled off! There are no matches anywhere—not that they want to lend to *us*, at any rate! Nfffff!

TRYGAIOS *aside:* Thank heavens for that! We're saved again!

WAR: All right: pick up the stuff, and come with me!
We'll have to look for some ourselves—and when we
find them . . .

QUARREL: Blow me! D'you want me to carry all this
lot?

WAR: You'll do as you're told, my lad, and like it!

*They pick up most of the kitchen equipment, which
is loaded on to QUARREL's reluctant back; then, still
squabbling, they go out. TRYGAIOS comes out from
hiding.*

TRYGAIOS: Well, what a relief! I never thought *that*
was going to work out all right! At least now we've
got an hour or two, before they find some matches and
set the whole of Greece on fire! This is your chance,
ladies and gentlemen! Come up here and help me now—
we'll need all the men we can get, to pull them out of
this hole! Farmers, carpenters, navvies, shipbuilders, anyone who can make it! Come up and help us now!

*In response to this request, the CHORUS begin coming
into the dancing-place. They represent all the states of
Greece, and are led by GEORGOS and AUTOURGOS.*

CHORUS:
Come up and help, all you who long
To find safety and happiness once again!
Come up and help, if you're tired of war,
And sick of swords and spears and shields!
Let the generals go and hang themselves—
For this is the day when Peace will come again!

GEORGOS: Trygaios, you'd better be the foreman, and
tell us what to do!

169

TRYGAIOS: All right: send some men for pickaxes and shovels, and get some long ropes ready to pull her up with!

The two leaders start organising the CHORUS, who sing a short ode as they gather all the equipment together.

CHORUS:
No more war! No more fighting!
No more trudging to the stores
To draw your rations: mouldy cheese,
Stale bread, vinegar-flavoured wine!
"Come here! Go there! March! Halt! Turn!"—
We'll never hear those words again!
For Peace is coming: golden Peace,
To end men's hate, and bring them happiness!

By the end of this ode everything is ready: some long ropes have been fastened to the rocks covering the hole, and brought down, ready to be pulled from the dancing-place.

AUTOURGOS: Right, sir: everything's ready. What's the next step?

TRYGAIOS *musingly*: Now let me see: where can we put the stones . . .

But any further activity is prevented by the angry arrival of HERMES.

HERMES: You nasty little man, *now* what are you up to?

TRYGAIOS: It's all right: we're only trying to rescue Peace—

HERMES: You fool! You can't!

TRYGAIOS: Can't? Why not?

HERMES: Don't you know what Zeus decreed? If we found a mortal trying to dig her out, he'd have to die!

TRYGAIOS: H'mmm . . . in other words, if I go on with it, I'm done for?

HERMES: If Zeus gets to hear about it, yes!

TRYGAIOS: But why *should* he get to hear of it? No one here would spill the beans, would they?

HERMES *grimly:* Oh, wouldn't they!

TRYGAIOS: Not *you*, surely?

HERMES: I certainly would! I've got a job to do as well as you, you know!

TRYGAIOS: Now look: be reasonable! Why should you tell him? Don't you want Peace rescued?

HERMES: Want? It doesn't matter what I *want*—I've got my job to think of!

TRYGAIOS: *Please!*

HERMES: No! Why should I? *(sulkily)* What have you ever done for me?

TRYGAIOS: I brought you a meat sandwich, didn't I?

HERMES: Huh! My job's worth more than a mouldy old meat sandwich! He'll tear me to pieces if I don't tell him! A meat sandwich! Hmmmph!

He turns away scornfully. However, TRYGAIOS *has another trick up his sleeve: he goes to the side of the stage, and comes back with a large golden libation-jug.*

TRYGAIOS: Well, if a meat sandwich isn't enough, will this do?

HERMES turns, and when he sees the gold his knees buckle slightly, and a glazed look comes into his eyes.

HERMES: Oooooh! I go all trembly when I get a glimpse of gold!

TRYGAIOS: Say nothing to Zeus—and it's yours! Now what d'you say?

HERMES *reluctantly:* All right: I'll say nothing! But don't *you* breathe a word to him about this goblet!

TRYGAIOS: No, no: your secret's safe with me!

He turns to the CHORUS—*but what he says is really meant for* HERMES.

Well, gentlemen, we can't fail now, with such a noble God as this to help us! Stand by with the ropes! We'll pour a libation, and then get busy!

HERMES' *new libation-jug is filled from a wine-skin, and he pours a libation, saying the appropriate chant:*

HERMES *chanting:*
The wine's being poured: keep silence,
And pray that the omens are good!

TRYGAIOS *now takes over, to propose the various toasts. As each one means another swig of wine, he tries to think of as many as possible.*

TRYGAIOS: Well, here's a toast—to Hermes . . . Peace . . . the Graces . . . the God of Love . . . er . . . er . . . Can anyone think of anyone else?

AUTOURGOS *brightly:* War?

GEORGOS: Don't be stupid!

TRYGAIOS *has a sudden inspiration.*

TRYGAIOS: I know! Quarrel! Let's drink to Quarrel!
He drinks to QUARREL. *But now inspiration, as well as the wine-skin, has run dry. Reluctantly* TRYGAIOS *puts down the libation-jug, which is eagerly seized by* HERMES.

All right, we'd better start! Are the ropes ready? Good: everyone take hold! Hermes, will you call the time for us?

HERMES: If you like . . . Ready? . . . Heave-ho! Heave-ho! Heeeeeave-ho!

But all their pulling is without result. At last TRY-GAIOS *drops the rope, breathless and disgruntled.*

TRYGAIOS: It's no good! Everyone's not pulling his weight! Let's try again—and this time *everybody* pull!

Once more they take up their positions. But now a figure in shining armour has crept in, unnoticed by everybody, and is sawing through the ropes with his sword.

HERMES: Heave-ho! Heave-ho! Heave-ho!

The rope breaks.

TRYGAIOS *disgustedly:* Now look what's happened! How can *that*—

He sees the man in armour.

Good lord, it's Lamachos! No wonder we weren't getting anywhere! Clear off, you! Go on, shoo! Shoo! No generals this morning, thank you!

He chases LAMACHOS *away, and the ropes are refastened.*

HERMES: Ready? One last try, then. Heave-ho! Heave-ho! Heeeave-ho!

But still no progress is made.

What's the matter with you? You'll never get her up at this rate! Anyone would think you didn't want to rescue her!

AUTOURGOS: Come on, you farmers! Let's show him what we can do when we really try! One last time, Hermes!

HERMES *wearily:* Oh, all right! Heave-ho! Heave-ho! (*with sudden excitement*) That's it! It's coming!

AUTOURGOS: He says it's coming! Heave!

HERMES: Heave-ho! Heave-ho! Heave-ho!

ALL: Heave-ho! Heave-ho! Heave-ho!

Suddenly the pile of stones collapses, and PEACE, HOLIDAY *and* HARVEST *are drawn up out of the hole. The* CHORUS *give a cheer, and* TRYGAIOS *goes to welcome* PEACE.

TRYGAIOS:

What can I find to say to you, my dear lady?
Where can I find a thousand-wine-cask word
To welcome you? I can't invent one
Fine enough to use, I greet you, Harvest,
Yes, and you too, Holiday! Oh Holiday,
You're rightly named! Your face is lovely, and—

He kisses her.

You have the sweetest breath! I smell the end
Of army service, and the purest scents
Of peace-time: ivy-wreaths and tankards,
Bleating sheep, women harvesting the grain,
Drunken slaves, pints upended, blazing hearths—
Every blessing that comes to us with Peace!

He turns to the CHORUS.

And you, my friends: do you remember the life
We used to lead, sheltered by our lady Peace?
Do you remember the fruit-cakes, the myrtle,
the figs, olives and doves, and the sweet scent
Of flowers growing down beside the well?
Oh, think of olives we long to taste
Again! What have you to say to her now,
Thanking her for all these joys?

CHORUS:
Lady, you're welcome back today!
The fields will smile to greet you:
The golden grain will bow its head in homage;
The forest trees, and whispering brooks, will sing
Undying praises to their mistress, and their Queen.

And silent lakes and age-worn mountain-tops
Will lose their gravity, and laugh for joy;
Our vines will bless you, and green saplings
Will bend their giddy heads for love of you.

For you, lady, have always been near to help us:
You have always blessed our gentle meadowland;
When the Spring flowers drive out Winter's snow
You are there, and the green shoots honour you—
Oh lady, you're welcome back today!

After this song there is a short pause. TRYGAIOS *is
clearly expecting some sort of reply from* PEACE, *and
when none is forthcoming, he takes* HERMES *on one
side, to ask:*

TRYGAIOS: What's the matter with her? Why won't
she say anything? What's wrong with her?

175

HERMES: I think it's the audience! She's so fed-up with the way they've treated her, and driven her out each time she tried to come back, that she won't say a thing till they've all gone home!

TRYGAIOS: But surely she'll whisper something to *you*, in private?

HERMES: Well, we can always try. (*to* PEACE) My lady, why won't you speak to them? Won't you tell them what the matter is?

PEACE remains silent.

Well, will you whisper it? Just to me?

PEACE signs that she will, and whispers for some time into his ear.

Oh, I see! That's what it was! (*to* TRYGAIOS) She says she's annoyed because you Athenians wouldn't have anything to do with her before. She came to you after the siege of Pylos, with a box of treaties under her arm—but every time she tried to speak, and end the war, you just threw her out of the Assembly!

TRYGAIOS: Yes, that's true enough. But we had no choice—at that time we were well and truly under Cleon's thumb, and didn't dare speak up for ourselves at all!

PEACE whispers once more to HERMES.

HERMES: And where's Cleon now, she wants to know.

TRYGAIOS: Dead, thank the lord: dead and done with!

HERMES: Then who's the new leader of the people?

TRYGAIOS: Hyperbolus!

PEACE turns away in disgust.

What's wrong?

HERMES: She's sickened that they should have chosen such a nincompoop to lead them! How can *he* help the city?

TRYGAIOS: I suppose they thought they'd been in the dark for long enough, as far as State affairs were concerned. Hyperbolus, being a lamp-maker by trade, seems the obvious man to shed some light on the whole business! Yes, they've sunk so low that they even think *that* sort of joke is funny! The city simply hasn't been worth living in since she left—and that's why we want to keep her with us for ever, now, and never give her up!

HERMES: I see. Very well: this is what you must do. Take Harvest, and marry her yourself. And present Peace and Holiday to the Assembly—when you've done that, there'll never be any war again!

TRYGAIOS: Hermes, how can I ever thank you for all your help?

HERMES *modestly:* Oh, it was nothing really! Any God would have done the same! . . . Er . . . Just remember me whenever you make a sacrifice—that's all I ask!

TRYGAIOS *looks around for his beetle.*

TRYGAIOS: Pegasus! Pegasus! Where are you?

HERMES: Oh, I'm afraid you'll never see him again!

TRYGAIOS: Why not?

HERMES: Haven't you heard? One of the royal chariot-horses went lame, and Zeus had to stop galloping round with his thunderbolts; so they decided to promote your beetle into the team!

TRYGAIOS: But how will I get home without him?

177

HERMES: Easy! The Goddesses here will take you! Just hang on tightly, and you'll be down before you know it!

TRYGAIOS: Come on, then, ladies—they'll all be dying of eagerness to meet you, down in Athens!

He shakes HERMES *by the hand.*

Goodbye then, Hermes.

HERMES: Goodbye, my mortal friend! And thanks again for the jug—and the sandwich!

He goes into Heaven. TRYGAIOS *and the three Goddesses leave, while everyone waves goodbye. Then* AUTOURGOS *beckons to the other members of the* CHORUS.

AUTOURGOS: Well, that's that! Now, over here, please, gentlemen. It's time for the Parabasis, time to tell the audience what a fine man Aristophanes is! You're sure you remember your lines? Georgos and I start off, and then you join in when we get to the Chorus. O.K.? Into your places, then.

The CHORUS *take up their positions in the dancing-place.*

Good! Ready, Georgos? Off you go, then!

GEORGOS:

When a writer of comedies comes to the front
   Of the stage to recite his own praise, it's time
For policemen to beat him with truncheons, and hunt
   Him from town! But if any composer of mime
Is deserving of praises (by God!) it's the man
   Who invented this play that you're watching tonight!
For although all his rivals include in *their* plan
   Aged chestnuts and musty old jokes, and then fight

178

For the prize with bad jokes about lice, and come out
  With the oldest of quips about rag-bags, or try
Hercules with his labours, or show you a lout
  Who's been cheated and beaten—(it's obvious why:
So another can laugh at the scars on his back,
  And say:

AUTOURGOS:

                      "My, you're unlucky! I see they've been
On parade up your back, and they've carved out a track
  Down your ribs for their army to march on!")—

GEORGOS: —and keen
Quips like these, which are vulgar and low!—

AUTOURGOS:

  "This was not how *our* author set out on his task
He threw out all the chestnuts, and tried to show
  How a *poet* can build up a play, with the mask
Of a comedy like all the rest, but not bad
  Like the others. He fills it with poetry, long
Words, high sentiments, jokes that are fresh.

GEORGOS:

                                    And he's had
As much trouble as Hercules, risking the pong
And the stink of the tannery, bearding the Thing[1]
  In its lair, with its mud-minded, jagged-toothed head,
And its henchmen, all hissing and threatening to sting
  If you touch them, its eyes gleaming bloodshot and
    red,
And its voice like a torrent of spluttering spit!

[1] Cleon. Aristophanes compares his own labours against Cleon
with the Labours of Hercules, one of which was to clean out the
stables at Augeus.

179

AUTOURGOS:

> Most men would be thankful to have giv'n him a
> miss,
>
> And kept quiet, and not angered the Beast in its pit—
>> But our hero, undaunted, went on fighting *this*
>
> To help you and your friends! Don't forget what he's
> done,
>
>> But be grateful: don't hesitate—vote him the prize
> Straight away! For our poet, whenever he won
>> In a comedy contest, he didn't set eyes
> On the praises of all the young students he met,
>> But he packed up his stuff, and went quietly home,
> Having given great pleasure to all, and in debt
>> To no other for stories or jokes.

GEORGOS:

> So we come
> Now before you to ask
>> you to give him the prize.
> Yes, it's clearly the task
>> of you all, in whose eyes
> He's so funny! We beg
>> all the bald-heads[1] to clap
> Him especially: reg-
>> ular stamping will trap
> Him the prize! In the bar
>> and at dinner, "The best!"
> They will call, "For our star
>> of the play! We request

[1] A reference to the fact that Aristophanes was himself bald.

You to bring him out now
                    all the titbits—we're proud
                    of our poet, and proud
Of his lofty bald brow ! "

CHORUS:

Muse, you must scorn all his rivals, and dance for our
    poet alone.
  For you have control
Over the feasts and the banquets and pleasures of Gods
    and of men.
Scorn poor Carcinos ![1] Don't help when he takes up
    his pen—
    Don't bless that played-out old soul !
" Come to me, Muse ! Join my chorus ! " he cries with
    a pitiful moan—

        But don't let him try to cajole
        You, and don't dance in his chorus,
        Slaves who come prancing before us,
Using what look like new dances, but aren't ! " Oh,
    no," you must say,
" They're not worth it ! " Last year he tried writing a
    play,
    And he even produced it—" The Mice " was it's
    name. . .
    Yes, but a cat got 's " Mice " ! What a shame !

---

[1] Carcinos, Melanthios and Morsimos were three of Aristophanes'
rival poets. Carcinos was an unsuccessful versifier, who was not
above stealing lines from other men's plays; while Melanthios
and Morsimos were as famous for their gluttony for fresh fish as
for their bad verses.

Then there's that glutton Melanthios, writing away
  at his plays:
    Don't help *him*, dearest Muse!
Also his brother, fat Morsimos, thinks *he* can write
  plays as well!
Tragedies, long-winded tragedies, sounding like something from Hell—
    These are the items they choose
    To send in for the contest. And then in the market,
    their ways
      Quite make me sick! When the news
        Of a fresh catch of fish comes
        To his ears, each one runs
Into the market to see what it's like: then they scare
  the old maids,
And ruin the stalls in their search for the best—and
  their raids
    Frequently fall on the poor! So refuse
    Help to these men, and join *us*, dearest Muse!

*

SCENE THREE

Scene: TRYGAIOS' *farmyard once again.* PEACE,
HOLIDAY *and* HARVEST *come in, and* TRYGAIOS
hobbles after them, rubbing his ankle.

TRYGAIOS: Well, I see now what they mean when they
  say it's easier going to Heaven than getting back again!

I practically broke my ankle coming down—it really is time they had that rainbow repaired!

He comes forward and takes a good look at the audience.

You've no idea how small *you* looked from up in Heaven! You were bad enough from there; but now I'm down again, I must say you don't look any better from here, either!

OIKETES comes in from the farmhouse.

OIKETES: Master! You're back, after all!

TRYGAIOS: Yes, so they tell me—and I've brought back these young ladies!

OIKETES *gaping:* My! Where did you pick *them* up? I'd never have thought they went in for *that* up there!

TRYGAIOS: Oh yes: they have to keep everybody happy!

OIKETES: Well, your trip certainly wasn't wasted, anyway! What are we to do with them?

TRYGAIOS: Take them inside, and see that Peace and Holiday are sent off to the Assembly, with my compliments!

OIKETES: And what about the other one?

TRYGAIOS: She's to be got ready for a wedding—mine!

OIKETES: I see: so *that's* what it was all about!

He takes the three Goddesses into the farmhouse, while AUTOURGOS and GEORGOS come up from the dancing-place to welcome TRYGAIOS home.

AUTOURGOS: Well, congratulations, my friend! How does it feel to be the saviour of Athens?

TRYGAIOS: Very nice—or it will, once I get this wedding over! I hate weddings!

183

GEORGOS: What—even your own? Take a look at the bride: *that* ought to cheer you up!

TRYGAIOS: Oh, it does, it does! But I'm still nervous!

OIKETES returns.

OIKETES: Well, that's settled. What next?

TRYGAIOS: Next, we must sacrifice. Fetch me the stuff out here, will you?

OIKETES collects all the things required for sacrifice.

OIKETES: There you are: one portable altar, one pot of holy water, one libation-jug, one basket of barley, and one sheep.

TRYGAIOS: Fine: I think we'll have the altar over here.

The altar is set up centre-stage.

Now, give me the corn and the libation-jug, while you fetch the carving-knife . . . Got it? Good: in that case, you can sacrifice the sheep—and mind you do it professionally!

OIKETES: *S-s-sacrifice?* Me? I couldn't (*with revulsion*) All that blood—ughh!

TRYGAIOS: You coward! Frightened of a little bit of blood! Here: give me the knife—I'll do it!

He takes the knife and goes boldly up to the sheep, which looks him straight in the eye. Pause.

H'm.

Pause.

Er . . .

OIKETES: Get on with it!

TRYGAIOS: Er . . . d'you think we really ought to do it out here? (*quickly*) Not that I'm squeamish, mind—I've sacrificed so many sheep I've lost count! (*With a hollow laugh*) It's just that . . . er . . . this is Peace's altar, and I wouldn't like to get it covered in blood! (*with sudden inspiration*) I know! We'll get the cook to do it, and bring us the meat out on a plate! (*suspiciously*) What are you laughing at?

OIKETES *hastily smothering a laugh:* Er, nothing, nothing!

He takes the sheep inside, and then comes back.

There. What next?

TRYGAIOS: Pick up the basket, and the holy water, and walk round the altar.

OIKETES *does so, going from right to left.*

No, no! The other way!

OIKETES *changes direction. The following instructions—especially the last one—are obeyed with great gusto as they are given.*

Dip your finger in the bowl. That's right. Now hold it out so that I can wash mine. Good. Now give me some barley, and sprinkle the audience with holy water! Done that? Right, let us pray. But just a minute! Where are all the pious people we invited?

OIKETES: There, in the audience!

TRYGAIOS: The audience? D'you think the *audience* is pious?

OIKETES: They must be: they didn't move a muscle just now, when I sprinkled them with all that water! All I

185

could see moving was their lips—they must have been praying!

TRYGAIOS *doubtfully*: They're not much good, but I suppose they'll have to do . . . All right, let us pray.

O fairest and dearest of Goddesses, Peace,
    Heavenly Queen,
Lady of dancing and happiness, please
    Accept our poor sacrifice.

AUTOURGOS:

Lady, accept our offerings, and stay with us!
The whole of Athens has come to pray with us
    That you will turn your lovely eyes
        On the city once more: we've been
Longing to see you, and take you in our arms,
    For thirteen years of terrible war!
Come out like a lady, and show us your charms:
    Bless us all as you did once before!

TRYGAIOS:

My lady, come down to us now from Heaven above,
And fill up our markets with all kinds of stuff—
    With garlic from Megara, baskets of fruit,
    Cucumbers, apples and sunfruit, and game that will
        suit
Every pocket! We'll soon see again
    All the gluttons and gourmets, all flurried and hot,
Getting jostled by fishwives at market!

GEORGOS:

                    But when
    That Melanthios comes, make him late
    For the market: let all the fish-shops be closed, not
A morsel left! And then he can say

186

Appropriate passages out his own tragedies, mournful and sad :

"Oh woe ! Oh far from joy ! My love's flown away
And been buried, in the frying-pan ! "—and bad
    Verses like that ! Oh, don't make us wait
For those blessings, Goddess—come to us now, we
    pray !

The prayer is suddenly interrupted by the S L A V E, *who staggers in with a huge plate of meat, which he dumps with great relief on the carving-table beside the altar.*

S L A V E : Phew ! That's better ! I thought when the beetle went that'd be the end of carting food about—and how wrong I was !

T R Y G A I O S : Have you seen to the Goddesses yet ?

S L A V E : Yes : Peace and Holiday have been safely delivered to the Assembly, and Harvest is being got ready for the wedding now. The cake's in the oven, and they're just trying on the wedding-dress.

T R Y G A I O S : Good ! Tell them to hurry : we're nearly ready.

S L A V E : Yes, sir.

He goes out.

T R Y G A I O S : Right : you start roasting the joints, Oiketes, while I carve the rest up over here.

They start preparing the sacrifice. But suddenly, after glancing off-stage, T R Y G A I O S *goes and says quietly to* O I K E T E S :

Don't look now, but there's a fellow with a laurel wreath approaching. What can *he* want ?

187

OIKETES *looking off-stage:* Good lord! He looks a shady customer!

TRYGAIOS: You know what I think? I think it's Hierokles, the begging priest from Oreus!

OIKETES: But what would he come *here* for?

TRYGAIOS: He won't like the idea of Peace—he always sells more prophecies when there's a war on! And he's sure to demand part of the sacrifice, as a reward for his third-rate oracles!

OIKETES: Well, what do we do?

TRYGAIOS: Best pretend we haven't seen him! Whatever he says, go on with what you're doing, and take no notice!

OIKETES: Right!

They return to their respective jobs. HIEROKLES, *a very tall, thin and ragged priest, with tattered clothes and a haggard look, comes in, sniffing appreciatively.*

HIEROKLES *in his best and most oily voice:* Tell me, brethren, to whom and for what are you sacrificing?

Silence.

You've chosen a beautiful day for it, anyway!

Silence. He coughs discreetly to attract attention.

Ahem!

Silence. He goes right up to TRYGAIOS.

Excuse me, sir: I asked who you were sacrificing to.

TRYGAIOS *to* OIKETES: How's the tail doing?

OIKETES: Magnificently, by Peace!

HIEROKLES: Ahem!

Silence.

188

Ahem! Aherrrrm!

Silence. He taps TRYGAIOS *on the shoulder.*

I'm a priest, you know: I'm entitled to the first slice!

Silence.

Are you deaf? I SAID I'M A PRIEST!!

TRYGAIOS: You're a perfect nuisance! (*to* OIKETES) Ready to carve yet? Good: put it over here, on the table!

OIKETES *takes the cooked meat over to the table, and* TRYGAIOS *starts carving.* HIEROKLES *peers over his shoulder, to make sure of getting the piece he wants.*

HIEROKLES: Er, there! No . . . there! That's the bit I'd like! That juicy bit by your left hand!

TRYGAIOS *to* OIKETES: Where's the dining-table? Bring the wine!

HIEROKLES: Er . . . the tongue's sliced separately, you know, in a proper sacrifice!

TRYGAIOS: I'll slice *your* tongue if you don't shut up! We're trying to sacrifice to our lady Peace, and all you can do is—

At the name 'Peace' HIEROKLES *goes slightly blue in the face.*

HIEROKLES *as if thunderstruck:* Peace? *Peace?*

He throws a " prophetic " trance.

" O ye redeless and foolish men "—

TRYGAIOS: Be quiet! You're spoiling the omens!

HIEROKLES:

" Ye are flouting the Gods—and I warn ye: ye've trusted

Yourselves and your property unto the fierce apes "—

At this TRYGAIOS *laughs immoderately, and* HIER-
OKLES *asks peevishly, in his normal voice:*

What's so funny?

TRYGAIOS: I like the idea of those fierce apes!

HIEROKLES *in his prophet's voice:*

 "Redeless and foolish, like doves, ye have trusted to
 foxes—

 Ah!

 They are crooks, with black hearts full of guile!"

TRYGAIOS *laughs so hard he forgets to watch what
he is doing, and burns his hand.*

TRYGAIOS: Ow! Now look what you've made me do!

HIEROKLES *in his normal voice:* Please don't interrupt!

 "If the nymphs cannot o'erdo
 Bakis, or Bakis fool men, or the nymphs fool lord
 Bakis"—

TRYGAIOS: For heaven's sake stop all this harping on
Bakis!

HIEROKLES:

 "The Gods are all saying the time is not ripe yet
 For peace to be made; first of all"—

TRYGAIOS *to* OIKETES, *in a prophet's voice:*

 "First sprinkle some salt on!"

HIEROKLES:

 "Nay! 'Tis not meet unto Heaven to make peace, not
 till the
 Wolf takes and marries the lamb!"

TRYGAIOS: And when d'you imagine a wolf will marry
a lamb, you idiot?

HIEROKLES: "Not while the beetle

Stinks as it flies, or the goldfinch brings forth little
  puppies !
Sir, you will never be able to make a crab not walk
  sideways ! "

TRYGAIOS *mocking him:*
  " Sir, you will never be able to fool us in Athens
  Now that Peace has returned—sir, you'll be out of a
    job ! "

HIEROKLES: "O Trygaios,
  You will never make smooth the rough skin of the
    hedgehog—"

*He is interrupted by a swift kick, and returns to his
normal voice.*

Ouch ! How dare you ! You haven't even got an oracle !

TRYGAIOS: Oh yes I have. It's one by Homer, and it goes
  like this :
  " When they escaped from the cloud of hideous war-
    fare,
  They welcomed Peace, and sacrificed joyfully to her;
  When the thighs were all cooked, then they started
  Pouring libations : and I led the way with a fine
    golden goblet—
  But not a drop did they give to the prophet ! "

HIEROKLES *scornfully:* Huh ! That sort of prophecy
  doesn't worry me ! Homer's no good—Bakis is the only
  prophet worth listening to !

TRYGAIOS: What about this one, then? It's also by
  Homer :
  " Cursed, heartless, detested is he who likes dreadful
    Civil war ! "

That means *you*!

HIEROKLES: "Sir, soon a vulture will join you

And try to get round you, aiming to trick and deceive you!"

TRYGAIOS: That's the first true prophecy you've made this morning! (*to* OIKETES) Pour the libation, and bring me my share of the offering!

OIKETES *pours a libation, to the accompaniment of the usual chant:*

OIKETES: "The wine's being poured: keep si—"

HIEROKLES *interrupting eagerly:* Come on! Pour me a cupful! And bring me *my* share of the offering!

TRYGAIOS *mocking his prophet's voice:* "Nay! 'Tis not meat unto heaven!"

HIEROKLES: I demand the tongue—it's mine by right!

TRYGAIOS: Go and eat your own tongue!

HIEROKLES *seizes the wine-skin, eagerly mouthing the chant:*

HIEROKLES: "The wine's being poured: keep—" Drat! It's empty!

TRYGAIOS *throws him a scrap of meat.*

TRYGAIOS: Here! Take this, and clear off!

HIEROKLES: Is that all? Won't you give me a bit of the tongue?

TRYGAIOS: Certainly—"when the wolf takes and marries the lamb!"

HIEROKLES: Please, I beseech you!

TRYGAIOS: Let go! "You can never make smooth the rough skin of the hedgehog!"

HIEROKLES: But what *can* I have, if I can't have the tongue?

TRYGAIOS: You can go and eat your Bakis!

HIEROKLES goes down on his knees, and clutches at
TRYGAIOS' legs.

HIEROKLES: Please give me the tongue! Please!
TRYGAIOS *exasperated:* I've had enough of this! Clear off!
Go and beg somewhere else!

HIEROKLES starts to leave, slowly and reluctantly.
But suddenly, as he passes the table, he snatches a joint of
the meat, and runs hastily off. TRYGAIOS is about to
pursue him with the carving knife when the SLAVE
comes out of the farmhouse.

SLAVE: Sir, sir! They're ready for you now, inside! Come
and change into your wedding-clothes!
TRYGAIOS: Well, I suppose we'd better let him go! Bring
the rest of the meat inside, though—it won't be safe out
here while he's around!

They all go into the farmhouse, taking with them the
trappings of the sacrifice. The CHORUS sing of the joys
of peace.

CHORUS:

There is nothing else that gives me pleasure
    Like a field just newly sown,
When the Gods in Heaven send us rain,
      And when a neighbour says:
"Come in, dear friend, and take a drink with us,
    While this fine shower comes down,
And God is helping us to grow the crops!
      Come in! Do please say yes!
Wife! Put some apples on to roast, and find some cakes
    And figs for us to eat—

193

And send a kitchen-maid to call the slaves in from
    The yard : it's far too wet
For them to go on hoeing weeds and pruning vines—
    Let's give them a treat
As well ! " And someone else puts in : "No, wait ! "
    Don't start your feasting yet !
I'll go and get those pheasants that I bagged
    The other day, and fetch some cream
As well—four pints we had, if I remember right !
    They're in the larder now,
Unless the cat has got them first : last night
    I saw her in a dream
Going foraging inside the larder ! But if
    There's any left, I vow
We'll all enjoy it ! Go and fetch it, slave;
    Bring three to us, and take the rest
In to my father—oh yes, and ask the gardener
    For a myrtle bough
To flavour this dear lady's stew : and please
    Make sure and get the best !
And while you're on your way, invite
    The neighbours all to join us ! " How
Gracious Heaven is towards us,
Blessing all our crops with rain,
And bringing golden harvest nearer !

*

SCENE FOUR

Scene: the same. As the CHORUS *finish their song,* TRYGAIOS *comes back out of the farmhouse, wearing wedding-clothes, and carrying a large, old-fashioned suit of armour, with a tattered but once magnificent helmet-crest. He is followed by* OIKETES.

TRYGAIOS: Phew! What a relief to get a bit of fresh air! What a crowd of guests there is inside!

He hands the armour to OIKETES.

Here: this can all go in the dustbin—it's not likely ever to be needed again! Just a moment, though! Don't throw the crest away: it'll do nicely for wiping tables down!

The FIRST MERCHANT *rushes in excitedly.*

1ST MERCHANT: Trygaios! Where's Trygaios?

TRYGAIOS: Here. What is it?

1ST MERCHANT: Oh Trygaios, my dear friend, how can I ever thank you?

TRYGAIOS: Thank me? What for?

1ST MERCHANT: You've brought me back to life! Business is booming!

TRYGAIOS: What business?

1STMERCHANT: I sell farm implements: sickles, ploughs, harrows, spades—all that sort of thing. Well, while the war was on, nobody wanted them: they just lay in the shop going rusty. But now! I've sold my whole stock in three days! Everyone wants to stock up, and start working the land again! How can I ever thank you?

TRYGAIOS: But what's it got to do with me?

1ST MERCHANT: If you hadn't brought us peace, we'd all be bankrupt by now! But as things are, we're doing better business now than we've ever done! (*confidentially*) Look—don't tell anyone, but if you ever want to stock up your farm again, you're welcome to anything in my shop—it won't cost you a penny!

TRYGAIOS: Well, thank you very much, my friend! Why don't you go inside and join the wedding feast? But quickly, mind—I can see one of your rivals coming in!

The FIRST MERCHANT *goes jubilantly into the farmhouse, just as the* SECOND MERCHANT *comes gloomily in.*

2ND MERCHANT: Oh dear! Trygaios—are you Trygaios? I'm ruined, and it's all your fault!

TRYGAIOS: What's wrong with *you*? Plume-onia?

2ND MERCHANT: I'm done for! My business is ruined!

TRYGAIOS: What do you do?

2ND MERCHANT: I was an armourer—best suits of mail in Athens! No one made straighter spears or faster arrows—and now: ruin! It's been weeks since I sold anything at all—and *that* was only a sword someone wanted to use as a carving knife! I'm ruined!

TRYGAIOS *musingly*: Look: I may be able to put some business your way. Have you any crests in stock?

2ND MERCHANT: Hundreds! But no one's wearing helmets any more!

TRYGAIOS: And spears—how are you for those?

2ND MERCHANT: I've got about thirty gross, going rotten in the stock-room!

TRYGAIOS: Good! I'll take the lot!

2ND MERCHANT *excitedly:* The lot? Thank you, thank you very much! (*eagerly*) You're not starting another war, are you? Please do—it'd be marvellous for trade!

TRYGAIOS: No, I'm afraid not.

2ND MERCHANT: Well, what d'you want all the crests and spears for?

TRYGAIOS: You've no idea how handy crests are for dusters! And as for spears—thirty gross you said you had? I'll take the lot: sawn in half they're just right for vine-poles!

The SECOND MERCHANT draws himself up, highly offended.

2ND MERCHANT: How dare you! I'm a craftsman, I'll have you know—and I don't intend my best-quality spears to be used for propping up vines! Good morning!

TRYGAIOS: Ah well, it's your loss, not mine!

With a snort of disgust, the SECOND MERCHANT stalks out. There is a discordant twanging sound from the other side of the stage.

TRYGAIOS: Good heavens! What next?

A MUSICIAN comes in wearily, carrying a battered harp, which he puts down with great relief.

MUSICIAN: Phew! That's better! It's no joke, bringing your harp to a party, I can tell you! It must be twelve miles from the city! I'm exhausted!

TRYGAIOS: But who are you?

MUSICIAN: I'm a musician, sir, the best in Athens—and I've written you a wedding-song!

TRYGAIOS *aside:* I'm sure I've seen him somewhere before
—and without that beard, too! (*to the* MUSICIAN) A
song, did you say? Well, let's hear it: if it's any good,
you can come in and sing it to the wedding guests.
(*aside*) I'm sure I know that face!

The MUSICIAN *tunes his harp, very inefficiently,
and then strikes a chord.*

MUSICIAN: I'm ready, sir.
TRYGAIOS: All right, let's hear it.

After a lengthy Oom-pah-pah introduction, the MUSI-
CIAN *sings, with a voice like a sick crow:*

MUSICIAN: "War, war, marvellous war!
           Nothing to beat it; nothing so glor-
           Ious! I've told you before:
           It's war for me—war, war,
           War I adore—"
TRYGAIOS: Good lord, stop it! What a revolting song!
How dare you sing of war *now*? There'll never be any war
again!
MUSICIAN *pleadingly:* Please, sir, give me a chance: it's
the only song I know!
TRYGAIOS: What? What sort of musician are you?
MUSICIAN *sadly:* Ah, I'm new to the trade, sir—I haven't
been at it for very long!

TRYGAIOS: I gathered that! Who are you, anyway?
MUSICIAN: I . . . I'd rather not say, sir!

He begins backing away. But TRYGAIOS *is too quick
for him, and snatches off his patently-false beard.*

TRYGAIOS: Good heavens, it's Lamachos! No wonder

you were singing about war! Clear off! We don't want
any of your sort around here! This is a peaceful house-
hold! Go on, off you go!

He chases him out, harp and all.

Lamachos, eh? Whatever next?

OIKETES comes out of the house.

OIKETES: Sir, they're coming! The wedding procession!
Are you ready?

TRYGAIOS: Yes: ready and waiting!

*A wedding procession comes out of the house, and goes
round the farmyard, blowing trumpets, throwing
streamers, laughing and shouting. In the midst of it, two
chairs are carried shoulder-high: one contains HARVEST,
and the other is for TRYGAIOS, who climbs into it,
with some difficulty. The procession begins to move slowly
off.*

TRYGAIOS:

Come, my dear one, to the fields
And join our happy harvest-time!

ALL:

Oh, happy pair! Oh, happy pair!

OIKETES:

Up you get sir: join your bride—
You're marrying eternal fame!

ALL:

Oh, happy man! Oh, happy man!

TRYGAIOS:

What shall I do with her?

ALL:

What will he do with her?

OIKETES:

Harvest her ! Harvest her !

ALL:

Harvest her ! Harvest her !

TRYGAIOS:

Onwards now in peace and plenty,
With nothing more to fear from war !

ALL:

Oh, happy pair ! Oh, happy pair !

*Gradually the noise of the procession dies away in the
distance, and* OIKETES *is left alone on the stage.*

OIKETES *to the audience:* Well, that's that, ladies and
gentlemen ! Why not come up and join us? There's
plenty to eat, plenty for everyone ! Just mention my name
at the stage-door ! See you later !

He bows and goes into the farmhouse.

*

PRONUNCIATION GUIDE
and
GLOSSARY OF NAMES

PRONUNCIATION GUIDE
and
GLOSSARY OF NAMES

Note: where there is a familiar English form of a name (as in Oedipus or Eurydice, for example), I have used that for preference. Otherwise the names are transliterated more or less letter-for-letter. Names not occurring in this list are pronounced as they look in English. In the list itself, the stress in each word is placed on the syllable in Roman type.

ANTIGONE (*An*-ti-*gon*-*ny*). Elder daughter of Oedipus.

APOLLO (A-poll-*owe*). The archer-God, believed by the Greeks to be responsible for plague and sickness. He was also the Sun-God and the God of prophecy, and had an important and world-famous shrine at Delphi.

ARTEMIS (Ar-*te*-*miss*). His sister-Goddess. She, too, was a huntress, famous for her archery.

AUTOURGOS (*Ow*-toor-*goss*). One of the Chorus-leaders in *Peace*. His name simply means " Farmer ".

BACCHUS (Bak-*uss*). The God responsible for vines and other growing things. He was also the patron God of Thebes.

BOEOTIA (*Bee*-oh-*sha*). A district famous for its poultry-farms.

CITHAERON (*Kith*-i-*ron*). A desolate mountain near the plain of Thebes.

CLEON (Klee-*on*). A tanner, and a leader of the Athenian people; Aristophanes was his bitterest enemy.

CREON (Kree-*on*). Brother of Jocasta, and later King of Thebes.

DELPHI (Delf-i). A shrine of Apollo, near Athens, famous as the dwelling of the Oracle whose prophecies were regarded as divinely inspired.

DIKAIOPOLIS (Dik-i-o-polis). The hero of *The Acharnians*. His name means "The man who wishes the city well".

DIKASTES (Dye-kass-tees). One of the Acharnians. His name means "Juryman".

ETEOCLES (Et-ee-o-klees). Elder son of Oedipus, and heir to the throne of Thebes.

EURIPIDES (You-rip-i-dees). One of the three great tragic poets of Athens, and a favourite butt for Aristophanes' satire.

EURYDICE (You-rid-i-say). Wife of Creon; Queen of Thebes.

GEORGOS (Gay-oar-goss). One of the Chorus-leaders in *Peace*. His name means "Farmer".

HAEMON (High-mon). Younger son of King Creon, beloved of Antigone.

ISMENE (Is-mee-ny). Younger sister of Antigone.

ISMENIAS (Is-mee-ni-ass). A slave's name.

JOCASTA (Yo-kass-ta). Wife of King Laius, and later of King Oedipus; Queen of Thebes.

LAIUS (Lie-uss). Ruler of Thebes before Oedipus.

LAKRATEIDES (Lak-ra-tay-dees). An Acharnian.

LAMACHOS (Lah-ma-koss). An Athenian general often satirised by Aristophanes. His name suits him well—it means "Very warlike".

LYKINOS (Lick-i-noss). One of Amphitheos' ancestors.

MEROPE (Me-ro-py). Wife of Polybus, Queen of Corinth.

NIKARCHOS (Nee-kar-koss). An informer.

OEDIPUS (Ee-di-puss). King of Thebes.

O I K E T E S (Oy-*ket-ees*). Servant of Trygaios in Peace.

P A I D I O N (Pie-*di-on*). Name for a female child.

P O L Y B U S (Polly-*bus*). King of Corinth.

P O L Y N I C E S (*Polly*-nigh-*sees*). Younger son of King Oedipus; brother of Antigone.

P O L Y P R A G M O N (*Polly*-praag-*mon*). An Acharnian. His name means " Busybody ".

T E L E P H O S (Tee-*le-phos*). A mythical King, famous for his oratory.

T H E O R O S (*Thee*-oar-*oss*). A diplomat.

T I R E S I A S (*Tie*-ree-*si-ass*). The famous blind prophet of Apollo, who lived in Thebes.

T R Y G A I O S (*Tri*-guy-*oss*). Hero of *Peace*. His name means " Harvester ".

X A N T H I A S (Zan-*thi-ass*). Name of a slave.

＊